Kathleen Devereux has been closely involved with children with special needs over the course of many years — as teacher, senior educational psychologist and tutor at the Cambridge Institute of Education. She is now continuing her commitment to this field in retirement and is an active member of the National Council for Special Education.

UNDERSTANDING
LEARNING
DIFFICULTIES

The Open University Press
Children with Special Needs Series

Editors

PHILLIP WILLIAMS
Professor and Head of the School of Education,
University College of North Wales, Bangor.

PETER YOUNG
Formerly Tutor in the education of children with
learning difficulties, Cambridge Institute of Education;
educational writer, researcher and consultant.

Both Phillip Williams and Peter Young were members
of the Warnock Committee of Enquiry into the Education
of Handicapped Children and Young People.

This is a series of short and authoritative introductions for parents, teachers, professionals and anyone concerned with children with special needs. The series will cover the range of physical, sensory, mental, emotional and behavioural difficulties, and the changing needs from infancy to adult life in the family, at school and in society. The authors have been selected for their wide experience and close professional involvement in their particular fields. All have written penetrating and practical books readily accessible to non-specialists.

Titles in the series

HELPING THE MALADJUSTED CHILD
Denis Stott

CHANGING SPECIAL EDUCATION
Wilfred K. Brennan

THE EARLY YEARS
Maurice Chazan and Alice Laing

THE TEACHER IS THE KEY
Kenneth Weber

UNDERSTANDING LEARNING DIFFICULTIES
Kathleen Devereux

In press
DEAF-BLIND INFANTS AND CHILDREN
John McInnes and Jacquelyn Treffry

In preparation
SPECIAL EDUCATIONAL NEEDS PAST AND PRESENT
David Pritchard

DYSLEXIA OR ILLITERACY?
Colin Tyre and Peter Young

Children with Special Needs

UNDERSTANDING LEARNING DIFFICULTIES

Kathleen Devereux

THE OPEN UNIVERSITY PRESS
Milton Keynes

The Open University Press
A division of
Open University Educational Enterprises Limited
12 Cofferidge Close
Stony Stratford
Milton Keynes MK11 1BY, England

First published 1982

British Library Cataloguing in Publication Data

Devereux, Kathleen
   Understanding learning difficulties.
   1. Learning disabilities   2. Slow learning children
   I. Title
   371.9   LC4704

   ISBN 0 335 10049 X (cased)
   ISBN 0 335 10053 8 (paper)

Typeset by
R. James Hall Typesetting and Book Production Services
and printed by Anchor Press Ltd., Tiptree.

CONTENTS

v

EDITORS' INTRODUCTION

In this book Kathleen Devereux examines ways in which we may facilitate learning in children with moderate and severe learning difficulties. Lucidly, with a wealth of examples and comment, she discusses a difficult area of great importance. The concepts of special educational need and of learning difficulties have been current for many years and have been placed in legislation in North America and this country. Here the 1981 Education Act, in its first sentence, states that 'a child has "special educational needs" if he has a learning difficulty which calls for special educational provision to be made for him'. In this book, Kathleen Devereux has concentrated her attention upon the difficulties and the needs of those seriously handicapped children who find learning significantly more difficult than do the majority of children of the same age. Her approach is realistic but positive. She believes that there is no child, no matter how severely disabled, for whom there is not some small, perhaps barely perceptible, step forward.

Kathleen Devereux shows us what these children's difficulties are and how they may be helped, step by step. However, she leaves us in no doubt that few generalisations can be made about them. Each is an individual with individual difficulties and individual ways of learning. Children do not all learn the same things in the same ways in the same sequence or at the same rate.

This is a story of professional commitment. But it is also a book which starts from a simple working definition of learning and then seeks to explain the process developmentally, drawing on many aspects of learning theory on the way. Gradually, piece by piece, Kathleen Devereux builds up a helpful model of learning and she concludes by demonstrating how we may use it in managing the learning of children with learning difficulties.

Perhaps most valuably of all, we may read the book as an account of how children like mute Andrew, deaf-blind and mentally handicapped Leo, immobile Mary, Jane with Down's syndrome, inaccessible-to-education Hassan, distractible Sally and many others have been understood and helped. We cannot read this book without learning about learning and about learning difficulties, without becoming more sensitive to the needs of these children, and without being better equipped to help and to guide them with a clearer sense of direction and a deeper sense of purpose. Above all, because she makes no extravagant claims and raises no false hopes, Kathleen Devereux succeeds in making us realise how much more we need to discover and know before the needs of these children can ever be fully met.

Peter Young
Phillip Williams

PREFACE

In a life which has been made 'various', to use George Eliot's felicitous term, by learning about learning I have accumulated many debts to pupils, students and colleagues as well as to my own tutors. Most must go unnoticed, but I cannot overlook the generous help of Roger Gurney, tutor at the Cambridge Institute of Education, whose comments on earlier drafts have been gratefully incorporated.

Except where the context makes it clear, every child mentioned in the text is a real person whom I have known. Although I have changed names and other identifying features I have tried not to distort actuality, and I hope I have succeeded. These young people will probably never know how much I owe them, but I trust that others, especially my students, will realize that I am well aware of my indebtedness to them all, and that I would thank them if I could.

Kathleen Devereux

1

LEARNING ABOUT LEARNING

"People whose lives are made various by learning" George Eliot

Parents and teachers who have the difficult task of meeting the needs of children with learning difficulties themselves have many needs. Among them is knowledge through which they can make sensible decisions with at least guarded confidence. Fortunately, there are sources of information for them to turn to, including books on handicapping conditions, administrative matters, the psychology and sociology of handicap and on methods of upbringing and education. Nevertheless, relatively little has been written for parents and teachers specifically on the psychology of learning with special reference to children whose handicap is a handicap of learning.

There are, of course, textbooks and journals dealing with theoretical issues and research. However, the application of these to home life and classroom practice is far from straightforward, and attempts to put research into effect are not always as rewarding as parents or teachers might expect or hope. Unless the rationale is understood (if, indeed, it is explained) it is difficult to know which piece of research is relevant to a particular case, and there may be a number to choose from. Consequently, attempts to apply findings can result in a fragmented approach. Both at home and in school this can lead to inconsistency and contradictory practices. Nevertheless, good practice is always underpinned by good theory, whether the relationship between the two is recognized or not. When parents and teachers are aware of this interdependence they can appreciate why a method works well, under what conditions and with what limitations. Otherwise it can be applied inappropriately, or modified in a way which cancels out its advantages. For these reasons a bridge is needed which spans the divide between theoretical understanding and practical applications, and an attempt to build such a bridge is the aim of this book. In particular, the subject matter will relate to the learning difficulties of severely handicapped children, but the principles have general application to learning, and to problems of learning in learners of all ages and at all stages.

Ten-year-old Philip frustrated by his shoelaces and Phyllis, his twin, defeated by knitting needles and wool are confronted by similar tasks: it is the level of difficulty that makes them appear to be different and this influences our judgements. Philip's problem is much harder to accept than his sister's. Feelings, in situations such as these, even when they are sympathetic, are not enough. This is one reason why the emphasis is being placed on understanding.

The germ of this conviction has been incubating a long time. Twenty years ago, after teaching for many years, I had the chance to study psychology seriously. While doing so my tutor asked me if I ever thought about learning theory while actually teaching. There was no alternative but to admit, unambiguously and shame-facedly, that I did not. In fact, he was not trying to humiliate me, but to test out the commonly held opinion that teachers use mainly skills and techniques that have been handed down and passed on, many established before the scientific study of behaviour became a separate discipline. By and large, it is thought, teachers teach as they were taught. Parents, likewise, reflect their own upbringing in the rearing of their families.

To say that this is so is not to denigrate either teachers or parents. It is good sense, in the absence of anything better, to use methods that have stood the test of time. Moreover, there is a great gap between learning in the laboratory and in the outside world, and no good purpose is served by ignoring this gap. When psychologists carry out a learning experiment they generally find out precisely what the members of their carefully chosen sample of the population can do, and then observe and measure changes in their ability to perform a specific, and sometimes meaningless, task presented under tightly-controlled conditions. Very often the conditions are varied in a series of experiments and differences in outcome are assessed by subjecting the findings to statistical analysis. The undertaking is circumscribed by well-established procedures. The keynote is rigour.

In contrast to this, when teachers say pupils have or have not learned something they usually mean that after some weeks, months or even years they can or cannot demonstrate useful knowledge or skill, or desirable attitudes or values. Thus school-children learn the geography of the British Isles, to embroider, to play football, to enjoy poetry or to be considerate of others, and teachers periodically assess their progress using the yardstick of expected achievement. They may, of course, conclude that what has been learned is an unintended outcome, confusing or undesirable, or a happy accident.

Some attainments, for example, reading, spelling and calculating, can be tested objectively, but even the best tests are fairly rough ways of measuring, not to be compared with the psychologist's stop-watch accuracy. It is the difference between the conditions in the laboratory and classroom (as well as the divergence of purpose) that accounts for some of the "great gap", for psychologists in the classroom are subject to the same kinds of constraints as teachers are. Many psychologists are well aware of this. At the Hester Adrian Research Centre,[1] for example, the specificity of a great deal of psychological experiment on the one hand, and the haphazard collection of information about learning difficulties from homes and schools on the other hand, have been avoided by using the methods of applied research. What is lost in precision is more than balanced by relevance. These methods also have the great advantage of depending on co-operation between research workers and "real" workers — the children's parents and their teachers. Applied research is itself a bridge between theory and practice.

An example of this is the project *Mentally Handicapped Teenagers and Their Families* (1977—1981) an extension of the *Parent Involvement Project* (1973—1977) which was concerned with younger children. The aim of the former was "to examine and evaluate ways of enhancing the personal development, leisure-time activities and social acceptability" of mentally handicapped adolescents through intensive work with their families. Parents contributed initially by corroborating, correcting or filling out the information which was gained from the teenagers themselves; by identifying specific problems; and by keeping diaries of the activities of the young people. Then, on the basis of all the information, individual programmes were devised and implemented at home and in school. While the overall planning, evaluation and dissemination of results was the responsibility of the Hester Adrian Research Team, led by Dorothy Jeffree, the Project Director, the procedures were carried out, at home and in school, as part of the day to day activities of the teenagers. The observation and video-recording facilities that the university provided enabled the parents and teachers to co-operate in the monitoring of the young people's progress, and kept them in touch with the project and the intentions of the researchers.

Projects such as these are recent developments. Twenty years ago it was perhaps to be expected that teachers were more concerned with techniques than with underlying principles. The number of teachers with advanced qualifications in the education of handicapped children was pathetically small and there was less encouragement to reflect on theories of upbringing than there is today. But change was in the air, and in common with many of my colleagues, prompted especially by my tutor's probing, I began to question and explore the impact of learning theories on teaching practices. It appeared, as should have been expected, that both in overall planning and in the minute to minute decisions which teachers are constantly making, my behaviour reflected my views about human nature. These were generally below the level of consciousness, seldom articulated and sometimes so vague as to be almost unrecognizable. I was guided by ill-assorted and probably inconsistent ideas.

This small essay into autobiography describes a condition which was, and still is, quite common. Teachers and parents are not necessarily bad at their job because they operate intuitively. Nevertheless, there are good reasons why implicit influences should become explicit and coherent. If teaching practices or upbringing fall short of what is desirable, intuition is unlikely to be sufficient to put matters right, by itself. Then there is the excitement of the intellectual chase, and the sense of security and of self-fulfilment that develops alongside deepening knowledge and self-knowledge. Moreover, as time passes it becomes a professional obligation to pass skills on to younger and less experienced colleagues and this entails awareness, objectivity and rationality. Parents may well find themselves giving support to others whom they meet in their local associations and for this they too need more than intuition.

One of the characteristics of human beings is the relatively few programmes for action with which they are born. As a species we have great potentiality for individual differences, adaptability and flexibility of behaviour. This can be seen in a class of mentally handicapped children as well as in a class of ordinary children. Although they share impaired capacity for learning they all stand with their own individualities and repertoires of habits, skills, knowledge, likes and dislikes, none of which are present at birth. Even the most severely handicapped children respond in ways that differentiate them from each other and adapt to their circumstances in their own way. This adaptability is one of the reasons that learning is valued, for uniqueness of personality is greatly esteemed. When information reaches babies through the sensations that impinge on their skin, eyes, ears, noses and mouths, they register and respond to that information. These experiences change their behaviour and these more-or-less permanent changes in behaviour are called learning. Upbringing in the home and education in school are the two greatest sources of planned learning experiences that determine children's development and shape their personality.

However, children do not respond equally to their opportunities. The rate, the amount and the style of learning vary from child to child. Some children, for example, appear to learn little by little; in learning to walk they may take first one step, then two and so on, over a number of weeks. Others seem to wait until one day they are not walking and the next day they are. Such differences are interesting but not worrying. Nevertheless, there are variations in learning which give rise to justifiable concern. A general lack of responsiveness, delays in development and what can, perhaps, be best described as negativism are the most freqeunt indications that all may not be well. When this is so, it is important that the child's behaviour is carefully observed and recorded in descriptive language, leaving interpretations until the facts are established. If these then show marked deviations from normal development decisions about treatment have to be made and carried out. However, this is not always a straightforward matter, and there is one particular problem. Diagnosis and prognosis are not perfectly matched. This arises partly from our uncertainty about the future consequences of present conditions.

In the days when a diagnosis of mental retardation meant that children would receive little or no education, a pessimistic prognosis was frequently found to be justified. But there were exceptions. The courage and determined efforts of parents and professionals demonstrated that intervention paid dividends. As a consequence the climate of opinion has been modified in the direction of more educational and occupational facilities for mentally retarded children and adults. For example, children in England and Wales who used to go to training centres have attended schools since 1971, and similar changes have taken place in other parts of the world. Consequently, such strides have been made in facilitating learning that it is unwise now to predict the limits of a handicapped child's development and long-term prognosis has become uncertain.

One thing we can be sure of: however disabled a child is, there is always a step, small maybe, and hard to recognize maybe, but a step that can be taken.

Leo was a 7-year-old, deaf-blind, mentally handicapped boy, the eldest of a family of three when he became the subject of a child study. Almost immediately he fell ill and was admitted to the children's ward of a general hospital. It was not possible for his mother to spend as much time with him as she wished, so the student, an experienced teacher on a post-graduate course, made sure that when he woke in the morning she was by his bedside. It happened that Leo slept on his back in a "hands together and eyes closed" position, and, since he could neither hear nor see the student, she enclosed his hands in hers when he stirred, to indicate her presence. As she moved them away she felt Leo's hands moving too. By a process of "leading", after a few mornings his hands were following hers to the limit of his stretch. This was the first unequivocal response that Leo had given her, and it became the basis of further learning. Moving his hands with hers was a step he had learned to take.

In the 'thirties a Russian psychologist, Lev Vygotsky, tried to untangle the complicated relationship between development and learning.[2] As a consequence he came up with a very useful principle. As he saw it there are some tasks that a child can perform unaided and some that could not sensibly be undertaken. Between these lies "the zone of potential development". In this zone are the tasks that the child can manage with help. With practice, these join the repertory of mastered accomplishments. It is for the teacher to facilitate pupils' learning by recognizing which steps they are ready to take, and to help them to take them.

This guiding principle is especially helpful when planning to meet special educational needs. However much or little a person knows or can do or appreciate, the end of the road is never reached and another step along the way remains to be taken.

When failure occurs it may be because the task has been unwisely chosen or presented. It is then the task or the teaching rather than the learning that needs changing. Sometimes children's learning styles are unhelpful. They may need to learn to learn. These and similar issues are examined in the final chapter, "The Management of Learning." but they need to be kept in mind all the time.

Moreover, it must never be forgotten that although in a book such as this the differences between children with and without special educational needs may seem to be absolute there is, in reality, no line that divides them. Nor are there any principles of learning that apply only to the handicapped. However, in the following chapters what we know about learning and related topics will be discussed, as has been explained, with reference to the special needs of children with severe learning difficulties. This is because such children need a lot of help from parents and teachers. Without that special help, as we saw in the past, little learning takes place.

It will be obvious that this is neither a textbook nor a D-I-Y manual; readers who wish for either, and both are necessary, will find that suggestions for further reading are appended.

It is fairly certain, based on the evidence of your sustained interest so far, that you, parent, teacher or other concerned adult, are among those whose lives have been "made various by learning". It is to be hoped that by learning more about learning you will be better able to add a little spice to the lives of your young charges.

NOTES AND REFERENCES

1. The Hester Adrian Research Centre at the University of Manchester was established in 1968, under the Directorship of Professor Peter Mittler, to study learning processes in the mentally handicapped. Areas of research have included language development, manual skills, personality, and environmental influences. The Centre has initiated services such as their pre-school project at Anson House and parents' workshops. Publications range widely, from picture books for handicapped children to scholarly works. The Centre has joined forces with other organizations and, with the Schools Council, has been responsible for a project on language and communication, published in 1979.

2. VYGOTSKY, L.S. (1963) "Learning and mental development at school age" in BRIAN and JOAN SIMON (Eds.) *Educational Psychology in the U.S.S.R.* London: Routledge and Kegan Paul. This article was written in 1934, the year of the author's death, and published in the USSR in 1956.

   See also Vygotsky's *Thought and Language*, Cambridge, Mass: M.I.T. Press (1962), Chapter 6. In the former the translation gives "the zone of potential development" and in the latter, "the zone of proximal development". Comparing the two suggests that "the zone of immediate development" is what is intended — that is, it is the identification of the "next step" that matters.

2

APPROACHES TO LEARNING

"Knowledge about the learning process represents power" W.F. Hill

When stone hot-water bottles were everyday pieces of domestic equipment a neighbour of ours had a son at the crawling stage who reached out and touched one before his mother could stop him. Thereafter she noticed that he kept well out of its way, so she put it, for example, at the bottom or top of the stairs where it served admirably as a gate. When as children we visited the house we were amused to see her using it to keep the boy within bounds. She took full advantage of an incidental experience which, had she known it, was an example of the simplest form of learning, responding to a signal or a sign. So simple is it that one experience, or trial, may be enough if the situation is sufficiently dramatic.

An overseas student provided another illustration. His young brother was just tall enough to reach the lavatory chain and as he pulled it there was a minor earthquake. He was greatly excited, and most disappointed when he failed to produce the same effect again.

In these two cases the stimulus in the first was a sign of fear and in the second, a sign of hope. Both resulted in emotional responses.

Because such learning has little bearing on the curriculum it is often treated by educationists as of theoretical or historical interest only, and most students are introduced to Pavlov's work, for example, as part of an academic exercise. However, Pavlov's contribution has particular relevance not only to animal learning but to the earliest expressions of learning in human infants.

PAVLOV'S CONTRIBUTION : CLASSICAL CONDITIONING

What Pavlov observed, when working as a physiologist, was a connection between certain events in a dog's everyday experience and its inborn responses, the reflexes.[1] The most widely quoted experiments are on the relationship between the amount of digestive juices dogs emitted when they saw food, and when they ate it. But Pavlov noticed that while the dogs were being prepared for the experiment they began to salivate even before seeing food. He therefore carried out experiments on ways of producing saliva by other 'unnatural' means (such as a bell ringing or a light flashing). He found that his dogs responded to these signals that food was on the way just as they did to the food itself, if at first the two were presented simultaneously.

Since then (about 1900) a lot of work has been done using eye-blinking, the rate of breathing and heart beating and so on instead of salivation. Experiments have been carried out both on increasing responses and on extinguishing them. Changing behaviour by pairing natural and artificial signals is known as classical conditioning.

REFLEXES IN HUMAN BABIES

There is another aspect of reflex behaviour in human beings: the developmental perspective. At birth the behaviour of babies depends on inborn abilities, and capacity for action is very limited. They have a dozen or so different reflexes including sucking, blinking, grasping, curling their toes and throwing their arms out when startled. Their early learning brings these automatic responses increasingly under voluntary control. By their first birthdays they no longer startle uncontrollably at a loud noise, but maybe will jump a little or just turn their heads to the sound. Smiling, which is initially involuntary, becomes highly selective and so on.

However, children who have sensory or motor disabilities, who have impaired reflexes, or who are brain-damaged, exhibit different patterns of development. Smiling is a case in point. The onset in both blind and sighted babies occurs during the first few weeks of life. This is the smile that mothers often attribute to wind. By four months sighted babies smile at those who smile at them, but obviously smiling by blind babies is not encouraged by smiling at them. Nevertheless, blind infants, in common with sighted ones, smile when touched or when hearing voices, and thereby show that they are using the opportunities for learning that are available to them.

Neurological examination in the first year of life of infants with Down's syndrome reveals deviations from the progress expected of normal infants. Generally speaking, they are more floppy (hypotonic) than most babies and cannot hold their heads up. Their reflexes such as grasping and startling do not disappear at the same rate. Automatic behaviours, such as making stepping movements when held so that the soles of their feet are touching a flat surface, also persist for longer periods, and there is a tendency for strabismus (squint), which is associated with general muscular weakness, to be more pronounced. This impaired neurological functioning goes along with retarded learning, a relationship which becomes more noticeable as the infants approach their first birthdays.

This is hardly surprising. The chromosomal abnormality which gives rise to Down's syndrome is associated with mental retardation, but apart from that, the hypotonic condition is itself a deterrent to learning. Babies whose heads still flop backwards at forty weeks, when they are lifted by their hands to a sitting position, have little opportunity to learn by looking. Normal babies who can hold their heads up and turn them at will soon learn to recognize their surroundings. They can hear footsteps and turn to see what is making them. They can view their world from many angles.

Two of the more reliable signs of normal learning ability are the way 10-month-olds use their first fingers and thumbs together (finger—thumb apposition) and point or shove with their first fingers (index finger approach). Babies with Down's syndrome, however, according to one well-documented study,[2] still flexed their fingers strongly around the examiner's finger, with a sustained grip for at least five to ten seconds, at an age when such a palmar grasp is not normally present. Only one out of seventy-six of the Down's syndrome babies, a little girl, had lost this reflex at 10 months: in fifty-five it was slackening but in twenty it was still fully present.

This has important implications when considering how young babies explore their world. Children who cannot focus their eyes simultaneously, and who cannot use their hands effectively, are denied two major sources of information about their environment. In normal development the hand feels what it touches and the eyes turn to see what it is. Later, the eyes search and when they light on something interesting the hands are outstretched to take it in, both literally and metaphorically. How else (except through the other sensory channels — hearing, taste, smell and movement) can "the outside get into the inside"? When babies do not use their hands and eyes (or other senses) they are not just disabled children but handicapped ones with very special educational needs. Their disability stops them doing certain things and their inability to do them prevents them from learning. If they cannot pick up their bricks and bang them together how will they learn the noise it makes?

In early learning a great deal depends on the satisfactory development of the nervous system. Neurological and psychological development go hand in hand.

Nevertheless, we become increasingly interested in what the child can do and understand, but we take the nervous system for granted.

However, if we are concerned about slow learning it may be necessary to take into account the possibility that the infant has neurological or sensory damage. It is important to appreciate the implications of such injury. Signal learning, which in an impaired nervous or sensory system may be affected, is the most fundamental of human capabilities, and a prerequisite for all learning, so that anything which interferes with it has far-reaching consequences. Moreover, it is important to realize that because mentally retarded people are, by definition, unable to engage in the advanced ways of learning to any great extent, low level skills are all the more important to them. We need to consider the part that signal learning plays in the everyday life of handicapped children.

Signal Learning

It may seem unnecessary to say that signal learning is what it says: it is learning to recognize a cue that triggers off associated behaviour. A signal is a directive, just as traffic lights or policemen on point duty tell the motorist to stop, or the steam from the kettle tells the cook to turn off the heat.

Many signals elicit emotional, not practical, responses, and they may operate below the level of awareness. It is unwise to generalize, but experience suggests that where reasoning and thought take a back seat, feeling comes to the fore. We could expect that the younger the child or the more retarded the person, the more their behaviour would be affected by emotions, pleasurable or painful. The characteristics of a signal are that they stimulate responses which are largely physiological or emotional. The skin may be flushed and the child fearful or tearful. These reactions are deep seated and often of long standing. Episodes can recur, seemingly out of the blue, but possibly more readily because of fatigue or minor ill-health. Early learning is persistent and, as Pavlov found, very difficult to extinguish.

Suppose a colleague has obviously got out of bed on the wrong side. You can react in a number of ways: you can keep out of the way; you can try to find out what is wrong; you can retaliate; you can remonstrate; you can placate, and so on. In other words a number of options are open to you. But suppose a mentally handicapped 12-year-old is totally uncooperative. The teacher's options are limited: it is impossible to keep out of the way and at the same time exercise a supervisory role; it is no good trying to find out what is wrong, for the child cannot explain; retaliation is out; remonstration is useless because it depends largely on appeals to reason; and placating is only possible if there is some give and take. It is tempting just to call the pupil stubborn (or worse), but what do labels contribute to changing behaviour? Is there anything the teacher can do, other than sit it out?

Since each case is different it is impossible to prescribe a cure, but it may help to recognize that awkwardnesses arise when children respond unconsciously to negative signals. Children are seldom wilfully stubborn (though some seem to be more so than others) and although temperament may be a part of the story it is not the whole of it. At some stage a stubborn child has learned, like the toddler with the hot water bottle, to be upset, frightened or resistant. Forcing the issue may make matters worse. Far better for encouraging signals to cancel out the negative ones.

It may seem that all signals presage disaster, but this is not so. The smell of frying bacon, a favourite dress, a piece of radio music may start the day off well, may signal to the child that another "beautiful morning" has begun. One of the attractive features of some continental schools is the habit the teachers have of greeting children as they come into the classroom by shaking hands and saying "good morning". This tells them that they are welcome and that the school day has started (apart from being a model of expected behaviour). Teachers can always find ways which suit their situation by sending out welcoming and other signals. And after a long and tiring day at school what is better than coming home to a table set for tea? Naturally, whatever parents or teachers do, children will, like adults, have their off days. This does not alter the fact that signal learning lies at the root of many of our daily routines.

From this we can conclude that it is important that the

signals we emit are consistent and reliable. Normally the sending of signals is as far below the level of awareness as the receiving of them, but not necessarily so. When we are responsible for the upbringing of handicapped children we need to be especially good at producing the signs they respond to. We need an exceptionally high level of self-awareness. We need to develop the skill of cancelling out signals of fear and distrust with signs of hope and confidence.

Avoidance Learning

The hot water bottle illustration at the beginning of the chapter demonstrates a disadvantage of using punishment in learning. Our neighbour did not deliberately burn her little boy. However, it is not unknown for a mother to put her child's fingers lightly on a teapot or kettle, saying "hot" in an admonishing tone of voice. Children certainly need to be protected from danger. The problem is that unless children disobey they never know if the teapot is hot or cold, or even that it can be cold. So learning comes to an end. When learning is rewarded there is no end to it, for every increment can lead to another. Fortunately, avoidance learning is seldom a permanent barrier to further learning. It is well known that switched-off electric fences keep out cattle, but only if they are switched on again from time to time.

Nevertheless, the persistence of early learning is such that fears may be implanted in a child and recur later — often, it seems, quite unreasonably. A child who is deterred by a gate from playing on the stairs until it is safe to do so is much less likely to have an exaggerated terror of an escalator than a child who has been taught to fear the stairs by being snatched from them as if from a lion's den. For that matter, it is sensible to carry a child until the strangeness of a moving stair wears off, just as it is wise to take children to the dentist before their teeth really need attention, so that the minimum amount of stress is put on the child (and the dentist!) on each occasion. What parents are doing is ensuring that when early signal learning recurs it comes as a sign of pleasure not pain.

Teachers, too, have their techniques. One is to encourage parents to bring children to visit the school before they are enrolled. Mothers are often apprehensive about leaving children with strangers when they know that they cannot make their needs understood, and cannot report back to them what has happened. Their unconscious signals of anxiety can be transmitted to the child; but if they can see other people's children happily settled, and the teachers' skills in action, their confidence is restored, and their signals impart their assurance.

Mentally handicapped children, like all children, can deviate in both directions: some can show too much apprehension and others can be distressingly foolhardy. In other words some children are temperamentally more prone to over-react to signals of fear and others to signals of hope. Some need more confidence and others more control.

OPERANT LEARNING

When we say that signal learning has taken place we imply that the child has learned to associate an event and its outcome or, in other words, to respond to a stimulus. Initially, these associations are conditional upon reflex mechanisms. There is, however, another way of learning by association. In this case it is not an association with a stimulus but with the consequences of actions, or operations, that is with the response that is made.

If the sound of footsteps is the prelude to mother approaching the cot the baby may be observed making anticipatory movements; this demonstrates that the child has learned to associate a signal (or stimulus) with its likely consequence, mother coming. If on the other hand the child associates shaking a rattle with a pleasurable sound the connection is formed between action (or response) and outcome. In this case the child operates on the rattle in order to produce the desired effect.

This is a very important difference, because it emphasizes the part the child plays and suggests an element of choice. Of all the possible things that could be done (kicking, playing with toes and so on) the effective one is to shake the rattle because it is this that produces the noise. Such a satisfying state of affairs increases the probability that the behaviour will recur. Thus the desirable outcome exerts control over the activity and the parent can say that the child has learned to wave the rattle. The psychologist expresses this by explaining that behaviour is reinforced and the child is conditioned.

Although there are different theoretical accounts of operant learning and reinforcement they share the idea that learning is determined by consequences. The after-effects strengthen the association or satisfy motives or, some such as B.F. Skinner[3] would say, must be contingent on the activity for learning to take place. These are the principles upon which the practices known as "behaviour modification" are based. It is not, it must be stressed, only through these techniques that behaviour modification takes place, for all learning modifies behaviour, by definition.

If a little boy or girl tips custard over his or her head the parent tells the rest of the family not to laugh or it will only happen again. If, on the other hand, the custard is eaten up parents indicate their pleasure in the way parents do. This is their way of encouraging the habits they approve of. It is the "law of effect" in operation, the law which states that a reward (or positive reinforcement) increases the chances that the behaviour it follows will recur.[4] On the face of it this principle is nothing more than common sense. Yet one sees, time after time, that "good" behaviour is taken for granted, while "bad" behaviour attracts attention. Attention may be just the reinforcement the child enjoys.

In one of the large psychiatric hospitals there used to be a notice over a ward door which went "Attention-seeking patients need attention!" Today this could be worded differently: attention-seekers need attention, but it is best given when what they are doing is worth encouraging. There is nothing easier for teachers than to notice the noisy, demanding members of the class and to overlook the quiet children. To some extent they have no choice. However, a bystander can see that the more teachers react to naughty children the more satisfaction these children get from their unruliness.

I recall seeing a teacher doing some language work with a small group of children, one of whom was a perpetual nuisance. The constant refrain was "Sit down Polly; Leave Jimmy alone, Polly. Don't do that Polly." Every time her teacher noticed her, it seemed to prompt her to further annoyances. In the end she was put out of the group, which should have ended the matter, but she turned her "punishment" to "reward" by sidling round to the back of the teacher and making faces at the other children which they greatly enjoyed. They gave her even more gratifying attention than she had received from her teacher.

The rewards given to encourage desirable behaviour can be smiles, hugs, words of praise, a treat such as a favourite occupation, or tangible objects such as tokens or titbits. The advice is first to observe the child to see what is preferred and then to use it as a reinforcer. However, learning is itself satisfying as will be shown in Chapter 7, but children may need to be shown what is successful.

Some of the materials that teachers use are specially designed with this in mind. The items in *Flying Start Learning to Learn* are a good example.[5] The first task is generally a four-piece puzzle — a picture of a familiar object, such as a house. If the pupil cannot put it together, a similar picture cut in two is presented. The teacher ensures that the chances of success are high by the way the parts are placed. In spite of this, mentally handicapped children may still have difficulty, but when they succeed their pleasure is unmistakable. The enthusiasm with which they tackle the rest of the two and four-piece puzzles, and later on the other games, leaves the observer in no doubt. There is a good illustration of this in the film, *Learning to Learn.*

It is important that the learner should know immediately if the response is correct. It is an aspect of the learning process that can, and should, be built into many classroom activities.

Aspects of learning through reinforcement

One advantage of learning through reinforcement is that it can form part of the general management of children, as well as the basis of treatment sessions. A child can be given specific tasks with planned rewards at regular intervals, often by a psychologist or other therapist. But the principles can also be applied to whatever the child is doing. The art is to encourage desirable behaviour as and when it happens, and to leave unwanted behaviour unrewarded. The omission of a reward is discouraging. This is what parents realize when they tell the family not to laugh at the custard-tipping baby.

Instead of rewarding children for doing right, they may be punished for doing wrong. A painful (or aversive) happening tends to decrease the probability that the same behaviour will be repeated. However, as was shown in signal learning, punishment is a general deterrent to learning, and should therefore be used sparingly. It is no use at all unless the child appreciates the connection between the wrongdoing and the consequences. Young or immature children cannot understand that they cannot go swimming today because they were naughty on the bus yesterday. If punishment there must be, the more immediate the better. "Time out" (isolating a child temporarily) is a recognized sanction, but it must really be "out" and must not be for so long that the child gets used to it, or the effect wears off.

Sometimes undesirable behaviour is reinforced because a child is able to dodge punishment (as Polly did when put out of the group by turning her teacher's aversive stimulus to her own advantage). This is called negative conditioning. It is rewarding, especially for the intrepid, and tends to increase unwanted behaviour. Children who manipulate adults have often hit on this kind of escape. They are quick to find ways of delaying going to bed, or of avoiding an unpleasant task without reaping the consequences. The more adults fall for their little tricks the better the children become at finding new strategies and exploiting old ones.

Recently, I saw a very undersized 9-year-old mentally handicapped boy who lives in a children's home. He responded to all unpleasant tasks by sitting on the ground wherever he happened to be, indoors, in shops or on the highway. His kindly house parents lifted, carried and petted him, without realizing that they were consolidating his undesirable behaviour. In school it was very difficult indeed to act as a countervailing force, for what started as avoidance behaviour became his regular and positive means of gaining satisfaction. Presumably, at some stage he would be too heavy to lift and carry. What would happen then?

His teachers, foreseeing the problem, provided him with a specially made harness (similar to toddler's reins but going between his legs as well as over his shoulders).[6] When he sat they pulled him to his feet, which was uncomfortable but not damaging. His sitting behaviour became less troublesome, and he learned better ways of getting attention.

Shaping Behaviour

It is a mistake to think that all learning is a mechanical matter of finding the right button to press or the right technique to apply. At best the methods already described only increase the chances that a specified response will be activated by an associated stimulus or outcome. There is no certainty.

In any case, every day life is a complex matter of interactions against an ever-changing backcloth of events. Children do not sit, like a car in a garage, waiting for someone to turn the key in the ignition. Nevertheless, the principles of learning through reinforcement can be both general guidelines and special prescriptions. Mary, a 9-year-old mentally handicapped girl with no physical disabilities, had spent all her life in an American residential institution. She could not walk at all. So over a period of eight weeks she was seen twice weekly in experimental sessions for a total of slightly less than nine hours. At first she was reinforced with popcorn, raisins and so on just for standing alone momentarily. Each session she had to stand for longer, and step further to get her reward. In the last session she took forty consecutive steps alone, and six months later was still walking.[7]

Since Mary was not taking any steps in the first sessions she obviously could not be rewarded for walking. What was reinforced initially was the slightest sign of standing, and from then on improvements in performance were given due recognition. This technique is called shaping behaviour. It is what parents do when they accept "ta", then "fankyou" and ultimately expect "thank you", except that parents apply the principle with much less rigour, since their training has to fit into ordinary home life not into experimental or treatment sessions. The important point is that it is not necessary to wait for the perfect or near-perfect performance: it is better to encourage any behaviour that leads towards the ultimate goal.

Andrew, a 12-year-old boy had no speech but he used a number of means to get what he wanted. It was reported that when much younger, and before joining his present school, he had had a small vocabulary. There were no physical disabilities, and he came from a prosperous and caring home. Retrospective case-histories are not completely reliable, but it seemed that his few words had been of little functional use (for instance, he could say "teddy", but not "more" or "can I have?") so they fell into disuse. Meanwhile, since he got what he wanted without speaking, it was the alternatives to speech that were rewarded. These included pointing, snatching and howling loudly. Andrew's behaviour, which was distressing his family so much, had been shaped, but unfortunately in the wrong direction. Only a radical attack on his conduct could reverse these habits. He was given ten minutes individual attention daily by his headteacher, with consistent back-up from his class teacher. When a breakthrough was made his family added their support. Sounds, then words, were established: two-word phrases were put together, and gradually longer strings were built up. The emphasis was on usefulness, but a systematic approach was also adopted.

LEARNING CHAINS

Andrew's task was to put together, in the right order, the sounds he was persuaded to make. These strings of mini-actions, or chains, are much more characteristic of human learning and behaviour than are isolated responses to signals or stimuli. Every morning that children get up, wash, dress, eat their breakfast, go to the lavatory, get ready for the bus and travel to school they are engaged in chains of behaviour, which are made up of many components. Each of these must be within their capabilities, or, if they cannot manage to do up buttons, brush their hair and so on, they must be helped over difficulties. While in school a similar process goes on, which is just as well, for if simple stimulus—response conditioning was the only form of learning human beings would be very limited in their attainments.

Chains are of varying lengths and of two main varieties. There are chains of actions, or motor behaviour, like cleaning teeth or building a tower of bricks, and there are sequences of words from "all gone dindin" to the verses of a popular song. Both motor and verbal chains depend on the child being able to carry out each of the individual links, in the right order.

Once again, therefore, the conditions in the learner have to be taken into account. The precondition for stimulus—response learning — that is, the ability of the child to recognize and respond to a signal — has already been described. The prerequisite for chaining is that the child has an established repertoire of individual connections. Thus each form of learning opens up the way for the following forms. The components of the motor chains include those activities that one sees young babies repeating time after time, picking things up, turning them over, dropping them, pulling, pushing, rolling, rattling and so on, activities which themselves may be short chains of behaviour. The constituents of verbal chains are the babbling sounds of infancy.

Unfortunately, mentally handicapped babies can seldom occupy themselves in these ways, for they are slow to get started on the road to learning. Nevertheless, before they can master everyday skills they need plenty of time to practise all the separate bits. These can then be combined in an infinite number of ways. This generally means that opportunities to build up these attainments have to be provided at a later age than is customary. What can often be seen is that because children are not ready to learn at the age when most children do, and because learning experiences are not presented at an age when they can benefit, they miss their chances all the way along the line.

Motor Chains

A baby's first movements are random and involuntary but they gradually come under voluntary control, with every stretch and bend repeated in every possible direction. These movements involve the muscles, tendons and joints which are connected to the brain, via the spinal cord, by nerve fibres. Since the brain constantly monitors what is going on in this movement (or kinaesthetic) system it is possible to feel the position of the body in space and to sense the movements of arms and legs, for example, without looking at them.

The experience of frequently repeated movements is essential. Anyone who has learned to play a stringed instrument knows that at first every finger has to be watched while it is consciously put in place. Practised players have left that behind them. They have built up a kinaesthetic memory bank of the movements needed for playing, and no longer need to look at their fingers.

When children start school without a healthy deposit account of motor skills they need to build one up. Depending on the severity of handicap, on age and on attainments, teachers plan an appropriate programme. The aim may be to improve movements of the head, body, arms and legs (gross motor skills) or the eyes, hands and fingers (fine motor skills). An important part of the programme is that which helps children to develop body image.

Developing a Body Image

While waving their arms and legs about, babies may knock their hands or feet against the cot sides and get a sensation of touch. This is closely allied in the nervous system to movement, the sensation of touch being initiated externally at the skin, and the sensation of movement internally. If hands or feet knock against each other, or some other part of the body, there are two sensations, travelling simultaneously to the sensory cortex in the brain. The two experiences, hitting the cot and hitting the body, superficially so similar, have this important difference that the former produces one sensation and the latter two. In a subtle way they enable the child to identify himself, to establish what is known as "me and not-me", and to discover the limit of his extremities.

In common with many others I have often pondered on why traditions are maintained, especially those that seem to be rather trivial. Among these are two games that adults play with young children, "This little piggy went to market" and "Round and round the garden went the teddy bear". They have in common an ending that involves running the fingers up the child's arm or leg. Not only the babies, but the adults too, appear to enjoy the games. Could it be that deep in adult memories are stored recollections of these pleasurable ways of building an image of the extremities of the body? Who can say? What is certain is that such an image is basic to many skills. How can you put your arm in a sleeve if you cannot sense where your arm is?

So, as a basis for the innumerable chains of behaviour that

we need for everyday living, children have to form a body image. It is relatively easy to see one's hands and feet, but impossible to see one's own back. Children who do not take what is behind them into consideration can be either clumsy or unenterprising in their use of space.

Parents may sometimes wonder why their rather large children are expected to roll on the floor, climb through hoops or tunnels, play on sag bags and so on, when they have so much to learn and so little time to learn it. But all these activities help children to establish control over their bodies, first by giving them experience of a range of different external pressures and second by challenging them to some special achievement.

The benefits of the swimming pool are often reported, for children who have access to one make progress out of the water, as well as in it. There are a number of reasons for this: one is that air does not usually make itself felt, and puts up no resistance, but water does. Jumping about in the pool provides total sensation to the body, not just to the soles of the feet, and is quite painless. Towelling down after being in the water adds to the experience.

In order to make the body image more explicit, names of the parts can be introduced. It is helpful if parents and teachers know what each expects and which words are used. If children in school sing the action song, "Heads, shoulders, knees and toes"[8] parents can help by saying, "over your head" as they put on the tee-shirt, and so on. The game "Simon says" is useful, because it can be adapted to whatever is being taught at the time. So are many finger rhymes and action songs, which teachers frequently adapt to their purpose.

A mirror is essential, and so are photographs. Schools that have cine or, better still, video-cameras can use them in movement lessons so that children can see their movements for themselves. This is especially helpful to children who ignore their backs, or who have difficulty in moving backwards. Whatever means are employed, the objectives are the same — to give children experiences that lead to the mastery of gross and fine motor skills.

Fine Motor Skills

When children feed themselves, use a pencil or a pair of scissors, or their hands for any purpose, they bring fine motor skills into play. These operations are not totally different from each other; they include combinations of similar actions modified and ordered in relation to the task. Many involve the co-ordination of hand and eye.

At first only approximate accuracy is acceptable: the expression "fine motor skills" does not imply great artistry or craftsmanship. For example, in the early stages of colouring shapes, outlines can be drawn with a thick felt pen so that there is a wide margin within which children can move up, down and across. As they become more skilful the width of the outline can be reduced. Tracing, colouring, cutting out, folding, and modelling all increase manipulative ability. Behaviour becomes increasingly flexible and adaptive and lays the foundations for more mature skills, needlecraft, woodwork and cooking among them. An occupation which is messy but valuable is finger-painting. The sensation of touch, added to that of movement, is instructive at the initial stages. Later on the less direct method, using a brush, can be tackled. The essential point is that chains of behaviour depend on the learner having the individual links and the teacher providing opportunities for practising putting the links together in the right order.

Backward and Forward Chaining

When the behavioural chain is something like putting on a jacket or tying shoelaces one way of teaching children is to start, not with the first component part, but with the last, so that they have only to complete the process. When they can do that they are shown how to do the last *two* movements; this ensures that they get the order right, that the nature of the task is clear and that each trial ends successfully. Gradually the children take over at earlier and earlier stages until they can begin at the beginning.

In a hospital school I came across a good example of this method. The older girls often made trifle for birthday parties. At first, the teacher did everything but decorate them. Then, having learned to make custard, the girls poured it on, left it to cool and decorated it. Step by step they strung together all the stages until they could start with tins of fruit, sponge cakes, jars of jam and so on — a collection of items that bear no resemblance to the finished article — and produce a creditable party dish.

Some chains are taught more easily in a forward direction. In this case, the first step is a cue to the second one, and so on. Breaking an egg is an example: handing over to someone else half-way would present more problems than it would solve. Therefore, the child has to be shown how to hold the egg, crack it and so on, and be given enough practice to get the hang of it.

Verbal Chains

The principles that apply to motor chains are equally relevant to verbal chaining. In normal child development single words are put together into two-word phrases, then into combinations of three, four or more words. It is advisable to follow a similar pattern when teaching mentally handicapped children to speak, though they may be much older. No child can put sounds together to form words, or words to form phrases and sentences, unless he has those sounds in his repertory, and unless he has models of language on which he can base his own structures.

Backward chaining in language learning is a technique used intuitively by many parents. They first say, "Pat-a-cake, pat-a-cake, baker's man" (using the traditional actions, another example of a simple motor chain) and go on to saying, "Pat-a-cake, pat-a-cake, baker's —— " leaving the child to fill the gap. Working backwards, the child can ultimately manage the line from the beginning.

Correcting Faulty Chains

Once a learned chain of behaviour is started the usual thing is for it to be continued to its conclusion. This is just as true for undesirable as for desirable processes. Because of the difficulty of interrupting the flow it is better to replace the unwanted chain by another one. The classic example of correcting a faulty chain concerns a girl who regularly came in and dropped her coat instead of hanging it up. Her mother remonstrated; the coat was picked up and put on the peg. This then became the chain of behaviour: come in, take off coat, drop it, hear mother's complaint, pick up and hang coat. A different chain had to be substituted, starting at the front gate. When she came in and dropped her coat she had to put it on again, go out to the gate, return and hang her coat up properly. She soon got the message. Dropping her coat was not reinforced and the desirable sequence of behaviour was established.

FURTHER IMPLICATIONS

Without a close association between an action and its rewarding reinforcement or between the links of the chain that lead to the desired end, stimulus—response and chained learning do not take place. If what happens one day has one consequence, and on another day another consequence, the child can only become confused and distrustful. For learning to be successful, expectations must be fulfilled. This is why teachers insist on certain routines in the classroom. To an outsider they may seem to be arbitrary and unnecessary, and, of course, an alternative routine might be just as effective. Haphazard behaviour is unproductive: it is not the same as flexibility, for the latter increases confidence and control, while the former destroys them.

Learning is cumulative. The more you have learned, the more you can learn. With the acquisition of a store of motor and verbal chains more mature types of learning become available. These will be discussed later. In this chapter the concentration has been on the early stages of learning because they are the essential forerunners of higher order learning skills.

The value of creating a firm base cannot be overestimated. In bringing up mentally handicapped children, laying foundations is a slow job, needing a lot of effort. The temptation is to press on, when to hurry slowly would be wiser. It takes courage to stay within the zone of potential development.

NOTES AND REFERENCES

1. PAVLOV, I.P. (1927) *Conditioned Reflexes*, London, Oxford University Press.

2. COWIE, Valerie A. (1970) *A Study of the Early Development of Mongols*, Institute for Research into Mental Retardation. London, Pergamon Press.

3. SKINNER, B.F. (1968) *The Technology of Teaching*, New York, Appleton-Century—Crofts.

4. The law of effect was originally formulated by EDWARD THORNDIKE in 1898 in an article on "Animal intelligence" and developed in 1931 in *Human Learning*, New York: Appleton-Century-Crofts.

5. *Flying Start Learning-to-Learn* is one of DR. DENIS STOTT'S learning kits. It was intended for pre-school children and children with poor language development, but has been found to be very useful in special schools. The kit is published in both the UK and North America by SRA, who also distribute the film, *Learning to Learn*.

6. This and similar aids for handicapped children can be obtained from Crelling's Harness for the Disabled, 11 The Crescent, Cleveleys, Lancs.

7. MEYERSON, L. and others (1974) "Behaviour modification in rehabilitation," in D.M. BOSWELL and JANET M. WINGROVE (Eds.) *The Handicapped Person in the Community*. London, Tavistock Publications in association with The Open University Press.

8. This song, and many others, can be found in *This Little Puffin* compiled by ELIZABETH MATTERSON, and published by Penguin Books, 1969.

3

LEARNING TO NOTICE

"Hello! Thingumbob again"   Wm James

In a school for mentally handicapped pupils a display table stands in the corridor leading from the hall to the classroom. In the summer various objects collected from a beach were arranged on it. On the pinboard behind it were photographs of children who had recently been to the seaside, some simple captions and questions in rebuses (see Figure 3.1).[1] While I waited to speak to the headteacher a few pupils walked straight past it, but then three boys stopped. They read from the rebus symbols "Are the little shells in the box?" They looked, conferred, nodded, pointed to the photographs and moved off. The children following them stopped and looked, or passed by, reacting in the various ways one would expect.

What can be inferred from this everyday incident? My impression was that although the display in itself was not sufficient to attract the attention of all the children, there was something about it that excited the interest of some of them. There was a chance for them to be involved in the display. The invitation to check the contents of the box was accepted, and the photographs were worth a second glance. It was tempting to speculate that those who passed by unheeding had not been on the outing, but as a chance observer I had no way of checking and had to resist the temptation to draw conclusions from insufficient data. What appeared to be the case, however, was that once some children stopped to look, most did.

Probably many people, including some parents and teachers, would be satisfied to leave the matter there, but for others this sort of event raises questions about the nature of attention and its contribution to learning. The importance of getting the attention

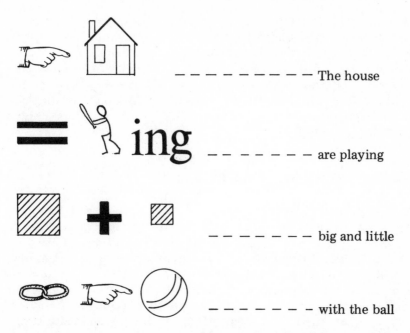

Figure 3.1 **Rebuses representing a thing, an action, attributes and a relationship** *From The Peabody Rebus Reading Program*[1]

of the other, and the frustration of not getting it, is a common experience, but in what ways do research psychologists regard attention? What questions have they attempted to answer?

From the 1920s to the '50s, very few, Until electronic equipment was available the only way of investigating attention was through introspection, a method fraught with difficulties and sadly out of favour. However, when electronic cameras and recorders, and sophisticated ways of monitoring neurological and physiological activity were introduced into psychological laboratories, the scene changed. It is encouraging to find that many of the conclusions which had been reached in the armchairs of nineteenth and early twentieth century pioneers were confirmed when unbiased technology was used. Concurrently, advances in intercontinental telegraphy, for example, raised problems which demanded research findings. The implications for education of these advances in psychological theory are considerable, but, in my view, largely ignored in the literature.

Meanwhile, observations of children with undoubted difficulties in learning have frequently revealed that for all practical purposes they are non-starters because the first important step, that of noticing, is never taken. Pavlov, it is said, thought there was no point in continuing an experiment with a dog that did not prick up its ears. Luckily for him, he could simply use another dog. Parents and teachers have no such choice. Instead, they have to seek out ways round the problem. This entails first understanding what happens when someone gives his attention to, or better, attends to something. Better, because attention gives the false impression of something a person has, while attending implies something he does.

SIGNAL LEARNING AND ATTENTION

In the previous chapter the nature of signal learning was described. One way of thinking about signal learning is to regard it as the attending phase of a learning sequence. This is the crucial first step for without it the rest of the learning sequence cannot follow. An event occurs and the learner looks or listens. The eyes or head may be turned or the hand outstretched. These are the overt signs that attention has been caught. Besides these there are changes in the automatic nervous system (ANS) which show up as alterations in the rate of breathing, heart beat, the EEG (electroencephalogram), skin resistance as measured on a galvanometer (GSR) and so on.

However, there is more to attending than having the attention caught. Attention must be held: the child must give his mind to his work, concentrate and be vigilant. This is clearly a quite different way of looking at the matter, and as it turns out, there are a number of different theoretical approaches, depending on which aspect of attending is being investigated.

One way of sorting out these different approaches is to separate two main strands of the concept. The first strand relates to the characteristics of the objects and events that attract notice. The second strand refers to the state of the organism, whether it is quiescent or aroused, sleepy or awake, passive or active. Thus, there are objective and subjective, or external and internal, factors in attention, and when attending takes place they both contribute and interact with each other.

Objective Factors in Attention

The attributes of the objects or events which have been found to invite attention can, within limits, be controlled by teachers because they can be introduced into the environment. They are an essential part of what teachers put into the learning process, for as every teacher knows, once the attention of the children is caught the teaching task is well under way. Alerting aspects of this input can be grouped under the general headings of contrast, novelty, threat and personal significance. We can consider them one at a time, before examining the subjective dimensions of attention, for these objective factors have implications for helping children with serious learning problems.

Contrast

The features of the environment that provide information do so by making an impact on the senses. Sights, sounds, textures and smells bombard the nervous system, which is also constantly receiving messages from within the body about the position and condition of its physique and organs. If all these messages were given the same weight the ticking of the clock and the beating of the heart would rank equally with the fire alarm.

There are, of course, situations in which any of these three, not only the fire alarm, impinge on consciousness: we hear the clock ticking when we listen after winding it, and also when the ticking stops. We are conscious of our beating hearts when undergoing physical or emotional stress. Changes in the prevailing conditions are registered: uniformity is tedious and we pay no heed to it, but contrast excites our interest.

One way, therefore, of arousing children is to present them with changing circumstances, but circumspectly. As in many situations, overdoing is as undesirable as underdoing. Only the judgement of the teacher can ensure that the level of excitation is appropriate. Take the seaside display mentioned at the beginning of this chapter: there were shells of different sizes, colours and shapes, pebbles in great variety, and seaweed and sand on the table. On the pinboard were photographs, captions and questions. Doubtless, after a lapse of time these would lose their appeal. The whole thing might then be set up in the classroom of the children most closely concerned, with a new arrangement and different questions. Learning takes place over time, and children need time to absorb new introductions, but they also need to be kept constantly stimulated. One way might be to get the pupils to help to rearrange the materials. Shells which had been sorted by size could be put together on the basis of shape or colour. In this way, not only is attention attracted, but it is directed to contrasting characteristics.

Rhythm and colour are both compelling and changes in levels of intensity and size can be put to good use. It is worth noticing that size does not necessarily mean large size. The tiny shells had their own special fascination. Changing the pitch of the voice, as well as the loudness of it, can bring back the wandering mind.

Desperation sometimes drives adults to raise the voice, but experimental evidence exists to show that lowering it is also effective. The important thing is to avoid monotony, and to keep shouting to a minimum, particularly if, for some reason, a teacher is in charge of a noisy class. In a noisy world it is quietness that provides the contrast. The ability to tell stories expressively, and to speak in character is certainly worth cultivating.

Movement is also alerting and has a focusing effect on the viewer. At one time it was quite usual to leave babies and handicapped children in cots with nothing to look at but the ceiling. Developmentally retarded children had no means of relieving the monotony. The colourful and sometimes tinkling mobiles now to be found in psychiatric hospitals, special care units and schools are there not merely to decorate, but to encourage the child who cannot literally sit up, metaphorically to sit up and take notice.

Further opportunities can be provided by propping the child up in one of the modern baby seats, or on conformable material such as sag bags, so that whatever, or whoever, is moving in the vicinity can be seen. A child can learn nothing about the mobility of things and people if there is no way of noticing that they are moving. This is especially important for mentally retarded children with additional handicaps.

The next stage for these multi-handicapped children is for them to be able to make things move by their own activity, even though the movements they make at first seem to be purposeless. Purpose will come in time. With a little ingenuity it is possible to fix things so that the unintentional flexing of arms or legs sets the mobiles dancing and jangling. This sometimes leads to the children deliberately producing the pleasing effect. Teachers have to be able to recognize whatever potentiality exists to be exploited and to take advantage of it. Some heavily handicapped children who notice few sights or sounds respond to smell. They will turn towards or away from scents that attract or repel them, thus showing that these changes in the atmosphere have been registered.

Preference for checkerboard patterns or face-like designs over plain card can be observed in very young normal infants and measured by calculating the amount of time babies stare at them. Definite and completed forms, in which there is order, are watched for longer than chaotic daubs. It is probable that this is also true

of handicapped children, but at an older age, and that they appreciate clarity.

The opposite of clarity is camouflage, the deliberate attempt
to conceal information. Occasionally, perhaps in an attempt to be
stimulating, classrooms become centres of camouflage. Overloading with visual display (like overloading with sound) can replace
contrast by muddle. Pictures of bonfire night, dinosaurs and trans-
port become a confused jumble. Some weeding out, and then
separation into defined topics, is called for. Differentiating devices,
such as the colour of the mount, or the size, colour and style of
the captions (if they are appropriate) help the immature observer,
because they direct attention to one thing at a time.

Sometimes contrasting textures can help a child to detect
differences that would otherwise pass unnoticed. Rubbing the
fingertips over sandpaper pasted on to board draws attention to
the shape, size and orientation of the cut-outs. The effect is
enhanced if children have to rely on touch and movement by
closing their eyes, or covering their hands with a cloth. (This also
applies to the identification of sounds and smells. Almost every
sighted person uses vision in preference to the other senses, whenever possible.) The activity can be turned into a game. The task
may be to find the nail-brush in the "feely bag"; the objective is
to attend to the relevant cues.

Novelty

Most children enjoy new things and new experiences, though
some handicapped children are disturbed by changes in their
surroundings or their routine. Probably most children (and adults)
find totally strange objects and situations unnerving. Generally,
however, novelty stimulates curiosity, and where this does not
happen spontaneously the child needs gently prodding or prompting, and praising for what is noticed.

What has been said about contrast applies to novelty, for the
child has to compare the present situation with previous ones. One
game to encourage this sort of attention consists of a number of
cards, on the first of which is a picture of a simple object such as
a cup. Each succeeding card includes an additional item, a saucer,
plate, knife and spoon, for example. A similar game can be played
using real objects and it can be made as simple or complicated as
necessary.

Regular features with older children can be "What have I

brought today?" Because lack of curiosity is so frequently associated with impaired ability to learn it is important to maintain a
steady level of awareness. Teachers who remark on a pupil's new
cardigan are providing a model of attending to novel stimuli.

It is not only unfamiliar sights and sounds that attract
attention, for children also respond to objects and events whose
appealing qualities they have previously experienced. Although
nagging induces apathy, some repeated occurences are welcome.
As advertisers know, spaced signals such as TV jingles or signature
tunes demand attention.

In the classroom teachers can and do use both familiarity
and unfamiliarity as ways of getting children ready to embark on
an activity. In singing and movement sessions it is usual to start
with a quickly recognized song or dance before introducing new
material. However, when the intention is to get children talking it
is a good idea to present a fresh object or idea to discuss. It is even
more successful if the background to novelty is neutral and
familiar. This is why setting the scene for the bedtime story is
important. Expectancy is an aid to attention. Both the opening
and closing of the school day should be sufficiently ritualistic to
signal to the child what comes next. Throughout the day, depending on the ages and maturity of the children, both novelty and
familiarity can be exploited, with a new rabbit produced out of an
old hat. "What's this?" encourages curiosity and anticipation.

Threat

One of the ways we avoid accidents is by making quick responses
to danger signals. Many of these are in symbolic form, hazard
signs on the highway, the flash sign for high voltage cables and so
on. These assume a certain level of understanding. Unless we can
rely on the young person being able to interpret the message we
have to interpose some less demanding signal. The last thing we
want to do is to make an inhibited child even less forthcoming,
but we have to safeguard the reckless. Sometimes the same process
serves both purposes. Kerb drill is a case in point. The timid
youngster can be given confidence to cross the road, and the
rash one prudence. We need to practise consistent responses to
the kerb edge and pedestrian crossings, signals of traffic dangers.

Until or unless we can trust a young person with corrosive
fluids, sharp knives and so on they should be in the category of
not-to-be-touched articles. Out-of-reach is enough for small
children, but insufficient as they grow taller. They have to be

taught to recognize danger. The guiding principles are simplicity and consistency, which implies parents and teachers working together.

Threatening events can have very marked physiological effects: the English language bears this out. We can tremble all over, shake like a jelly, go white as a sheet, feel the blood run cold, or our hair stand on end. Fright can chill the spine, make our flesh creep, our knees knock together or our teeth chatter. None of these are reactions we want to see in children who already find life difficult enough. This is why threat, as a means of gaining attention, should be a last resort, and, if possible, avoided altogether.

Personal Significance

Attentive behaviour, in common with all behaviour, can be increased or diminished through experience. Attributes of objects or events compel children to look, listen, smell, taste or touch, but not equally. What excites interest in one child may leave another one unmoved. As soon as the learning process begins some items in the environment come to have more significance than others. Among these are one's own name; this is a common feature of our personal selection of things to notice. Selection is an important aspect of attention. To make life interesting we select what to attend to and, to make it manageable, what not to attend to. Selective attention implies selective inattention.

When we consider what makes some elements in the total environment stand out, and others not, we cross the ill-defined borderlines between the objective and subjective factors in attention, and between attention and perception. Memory, too, must be involved for unless present and past signals can be compared there can be no recognition. We attend most assiduously to what we recognize from previous experience to be worth the effort.

Subjective Factors in Attention

There is a paradox here, for it is said that attention is paid on the one hand to new experiences and on the other to those whose importance has been learned already. There are a number of possible explanations; one which is generally accepted goes like this. Sensations are converted into sensory impulses which travel along the nerve fibres to the cortex, the developed part of the brain that is concerned with learning and thinking (the grey matter) and to the brain stem. In the brain stem the impulses pass through a dense network of fibres, a relay centre, known as the

Ascending Reticular Activating System or ARAS.[2] The purpose of the ARAS is to heighten or damp down the level of arousal or alertness. Thus in sleep many signals are turned down, whereas in dangerous or exciting situations they are intensified. These effects occur through the passage of impulses between the cortex and the ARAS. It is as though the cortex tells the relay centre "I don't recognize this: turn up my volume control" or "I remember this: better watch out" or vice versa. Then the ARAS increases or decreases the strength of the impulses (see Figure 3.2).

In all cases the level of alertness is determined by the response of the brain to the impulses it receives. At the same time the brain stem network regulates certain bodily functions. Thus both the body and the mind are alert or drowsy so that the child is ready to notice, or not notice, as the case may be.

Alertness

When children (or adults) are drowsy they are less capable of paying attention than when fully awake and since there is a mid-afternoon drop in arousal level it is unwise to present tasks which require considerable concentration at this time. In general, bodily discomfort makes it difficult to concentrate so being neither too hot nor too cold, nor hungry or thirsty is advisable. Very young babies, whose waking periods are short, are sometimes most alert immediately after being fed. It is worth while observing young handicapped children to see at what times of the day they are most responsive, for the attender must be active and searching. Attention is never passive.

Developmental Aspects

As children grow older they spend increasing proportions of their time awake and active, and their capacity for sustained attention improves. In normally developing children there is a marked change round about 8 to 9 years of age, which can be seen not only in their everyday behaviour, but also on their EEGs, which begin to show adult patterns of arousal. This corresponds with the ability of pupils in school to stay interested in tasks which cannot be completed immediately, a stage which may not be reached by handicapped pupils until they are in their late teens.

Besides these changes in their capacity to remain attentive there are age trends associated with the selection of features to notice. Before a child can carry out a discrimination task, for

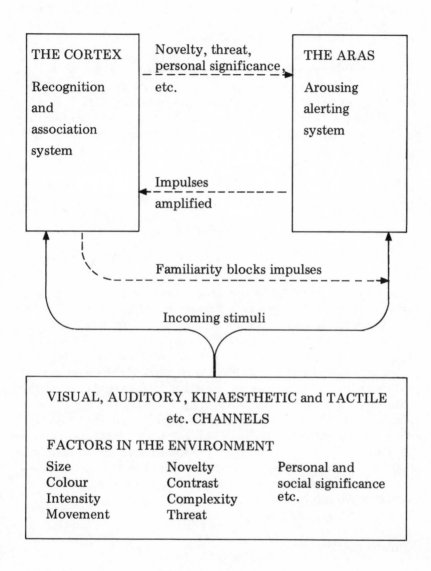

Figure 3.2 A model of attention Incoming stimuli follow neural pathways to the cortex and the ARAS. If the stimulus is familiar the cortex sends an inhibiting message to the ARAS but when it is recognized as novel, threatening or exciting etc. the impulses from the cortex to the ARAS have the effect of amplifying the impulses that travel back from the ARAS to the cortex. The activity of the ARAS is necessary for consciousness

example sorting objects by size, colour or shape, a decision has to be made (frequently unconsciously) whether size, colour or shape is relevant. If rewarded for choosing a red square instead of a green circle the child cannot tell if the redness or squareness was significant. Immature children tend to go for shape. It is only as they grow older that they can switch their choice to another shape, and changing from shape to colour comes later still. This is another way of saying that some handicapped children's behaviour tends to be rigid. When children cannot shift their attention readily, either to another dimension as from form to colour, or from one cue to another as from square to triangle or yellow to blue, their learning is inhibited at source, for paying attention to the relevant dimension and the cues within that dimension is the first step in the learning process.[3]

Purpose

When confronted with a mass of information from which some needs to be selected, such as a picture full of detail, the effective attender scans it systematically and purposefully. Unfortunately, this is not the case with mentally retarded children, who, as has been shown above, tend to fix on one aspect, not always the most productive one, or to flit haphazardly. Such children need to be prompted to attend to relevant cues and to play games in which a systematic approach is inherent. The "learning to learn" games mentioned in Chapter 2 include this feature, and as the children know immediately if they have made a mistake self-correction is built in. P.E. lessons are also useful settings for encouraging sustained activity. Keeping a balloon in the air, for example, demands constant attention,and crawling through a tunnel, once started, really has to be completed.

Reactive Inhibition

If the signals which give rise to the impulses are unvaried they become as wallpaper, or the incessant hum of city noises, that is, unnoticed. Monotony is not just boring: it is physiologically impossible to stay aroused if the sensory impulses reaching the brain stem and the cortex are unchanging. There is a limit to vigilance. Try watching toast! In the classroom it means that no display, however good, will be noticed indefinitely. It also means that it is difficult for children to keep up a steady standard of performance in a repetitive task, unless some variety is introduced into it.

In this, as in all human activity, there is a range of behaviour. Some children can concentrate on repetitive tasks for longer than others; some switch off very quickly, others seem almost unable to do so. The differences may be inherent. In some cases it may be that drugs affect the activity in the brain stem, and therefore the child's general alertness. The child may be unusually sluggish or so restless that there is no time to settle to anything. The slightest thing is distracting.

Distractability

When children flit purposelessly from one thing to another they are said to be distractable, overactive or hyperactive. Some years ago, researchers suggested relieving such children of the strain of ignoring unwanted stimuli by giving them sound-proof cubicles with blank walls (like voting station booths) during "learning" sessions. If all extraneous happenings took their minds off their work, then why not try getting rid of the distractions? It seemed a good idea.

However, even very distractable children do not react to the aspects of their environment that are familiar and constant. What catches their eyes and ears is change, and for some of them completely unstimulating surroundings seem to be an upsetting alteration in their situation.

So what can be done? Occasionally children themselves suggest a lead. Molly, a mildly spastic, moderately retarded 9-year-old went off on her own so frequently that her teacher was worried and referred her to the School Psychological Service. I knew her as a friendly child, with understanding, supportive parents, and was surprised to hear that she might be emotionally disturbed. However, I went to see what was happening.

In the playground and on social occasions in the classroom, shopping games for instance, Molly seemed quite at ease, and a happy child. Nevertheless, the teacher's observation was confirmed. When given individual work to do Molly retired to a table by the wall where she had made a small study, with her belongings round her, and her back to the classroom activities. It looked as though, in an atmosphere of disciplined freedom, she had found an ideal workplace for herself, not stimulus-free, but undemanding.

Since then, there has been research evidence to suggest that some brain-injured children need surroundings so familiar to them that there is no compulsion to react to them. They can then give their minds to the task in hand. More recently still researchers have looked at the possibility that some children are overactive because that is the only way they can get enough stimulation. If this is so they need an intensification of classroom richness, not a reduction. Such children should be given a programme of diverse activities, which include plenty of movement, colour and sound.[4]

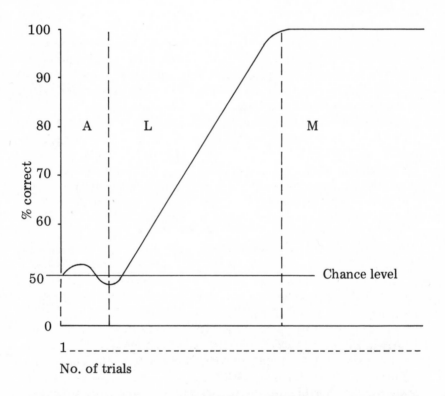

Figure 3.3a   A simulated learning curve   In this graph of children's performances on button-sorting tasks one can see that very few trials were needed to learn which dimensions and cues (colour, size etc.) were relevant — the attention phase, A. Then in succeeding tests the number of buttons correctly sorted increased during the learning phase, L, until mastery, M, was reached.

ATTENTION AND LEARNING

One finding which has not yet been mentioned is of particular interest to teachers of children with learning difficulties. When children of ordinary ability learn to do something for the first time their early attempts are often faulty, but with steady improvement they reach an acceptable standard of performance. If their efforts range from a fifty—fifty chance of being correct to being right every time they can be plotted on a graph as in Figure 3.3a. If mentally handicapped children are given a new task to learn their progress is as in Figure 3.3b. The interesting thing is that if

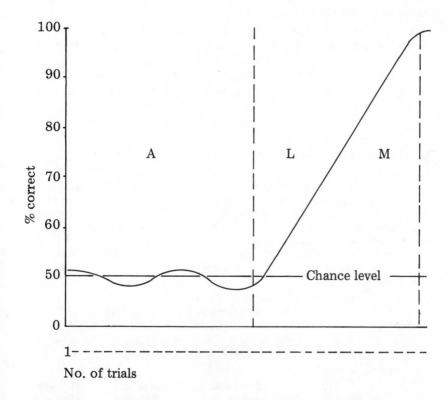

Figure 3.3b   A simulated backward learning curve   In this graph of mentally handicapped children's performances on button-sorting tasks one can see that many trials were needed before they were able to identify relevant dimensions and cues. There is a prolonged attention phase, A, at the chance, or guessing, level with a 50—50 probability of being correct. But then the time taken to sort correctly corresponds to that in Figure 3.3a, and the learning curve of 3.3b if moved backwards would overlay that of 3.3a. The difference lies specifically in the "getting started" or attention phase

3.3b is superimposed on 3.3a and moved backwards, the curves are the same.[5] What has happened is that the handicapped children have taken much longer to get started, but have then improved at a rate similar to that of normal children. This, of course, is only true if the tasks are within the ability of both groups. In experimental work sorting tasks are often given because the results can be easily graded. It is thought that handicapped children are slow to get started because they do not know what to attend to: this is a problem which comes up for consideration time and time again.

In this chapter, attention has been discussed in terms of what the child assimilates from the environment. When we come to think about learning skills we shall see that children can also pay attention to the response they intend to make. Being prepared to catch a ball is manifested in the position the body, arms and hands take up. Getting set, and ready to go is a way of attending.

Attention is the first phase of the learning sequence. It is important because without it nothing follows. However, it is also necessary to make sense of what is noticed. This is what the next chapter is about.

NOTES AND REFERENCES

1. The *Peabody Rebus Reading Program* (REBUS) is a method of introducing reading using pictorial, geometric and abstract symbols instead of spelled words. It has been found to be a useful adjunct to language development programmes for mentally handicapped children, some of whom have made the transition to "real" reading. Distributors are Educational Evaluation Enterprises, Awre, Newnham, Gloucestershire, GL14 1ET, and American Guidance Services Inc., Circle Pines, Minnesota 55014.

2. A good account of the interaction between the cortex and the ARAS can be found in *Pathology of Attention* by A. McGHIE, published in Penguin Science of Behaviour Books, 1969.

3. ZEAMAN, D. and HOUSE, Betty J. (1979) 'A review of attention theory' in N.R. Ellis (Ed.) *Handbook of Mental Deficiency*, 2nd ed., New Jersey: Lawrence Erlbaum Associates.

4. BOWERS, A. (1980) "An educational management approach to hyperactive behaviour in the classroom", *Remedial Education*, Vol. 15, No. 1.

5. ZEAMAN, D. and HOUSE, Betty J. (1963) "The role of attention in retardate discrimination learning", in N.R. ELLIS (Ed.) *Handbook of Mental Deficiency* New York: McGraw Hill. In their more recent contribution "A review of attention theory" in the 2nd edition (1979) the findings reported in 1963 have been elaborated.

4

THE WELL-TRODDEN PATHWAYS

"Knowledge brings foresight"   G.P. Meredith

A common characteristic of many of the everyday activities of adults is the little conscious effort that goes into performing them. We may need to make decisions about what to wear, or to eat, or where to go, but not how to put our clothes on, handle cutlery or open the door. We perform these sorts of automatic actions without giving them a second thought. In fact, it is difficult to do some of them except automatically, so firmly established are the necessary sequences of movements.

At the time these automations were acquired this was not so. For example, adults turn the pages of a book effortlessly but young children have to give the same action their concentrated attention, and may even need a number of trials before they succeed. Adults, too, embarking on a fresh skill, such as playing a guitar, may be very clumsy in their early attempts. However, both children and adults, in the process of acquiring new skills, get to know a little more of the world they live in, and the qualities of the materials they are manipulating. They develop a notion of what is going on.

Both the actions and notions are sometimes called "schemata" (the singular is schema). One of the frustrating aspects of teaching mentally handicapped children is the feeling that everything has to be taught from scratch. A child who can put a jacket on may not be able to manage a coat: the movements have been mastered, but the idea behind them is not assimilated.

THE CONCEPT OF THE SCHEMA

What is implied by the possession of schemata? It is that there are patterns of brain activity which are stimulated by nerve impulses to produce images, and at the same time patterns of brain activity which result in interpretations of the images. Saying that human beings can interpret objects and events is another way of saying that they can make sense of them.

It is misleading to envisage images as a sort of microfilm in the brain, or the mind as a collection of bits, building blocks if you like, or jigsaw puzzle pieces. There is no adequate analogy: it may be helpful for all that (as Professor Meredith suggested) to think of schemata as currents in an ocean, or the music of an orchestra.[1] Schemata overlap, and one idea leads to and intertwines with another. What is implied by the possession of schemata is that something is going on in the child's brain which is not fully explained by an observer identifying stimuli and responses. The mind, we say, is working.

Both images and interpretations form, develop, and re-form. Without use they perish, and every individual assembles a unique pattern of schemata, organized, over shorter or longer periods, as a consequence of personal experiences. We live in a changing world and we bring to our knowledge of it our own selection of significant features.

The way in which learning is being described (because only one thing can be dealt with at a time) might suggest that children go through stages of signal learning, then instrumental learning, then chaining and then begin to develop schemata. This is not the case. Each is a prerequisite of succeeding kinds of performance, but the earlier kinds continue to play their part alongside the higher activities. Moreover, chaining can range from simple to complex sequences, and schemata, as we shall see, are built up throughout life and can also exist at many levels.

Organizing at the Integrative Level

If the reflexes of sucking and grasping are present at birth, these innate patterns of behaviour, together with gross bodily activity, immediately bring the baby into active contact with the environment. At first sucking, for example, occurs whenever anything touches the baby's mouth, and can even be observed in the sleeping baby. Babies also grasp objects and frequently bring their hands to their mouths. By this means, thumbs, corners of blankets and other unnourishing objects can be investigated by the infant. For many months babies employ their lips for getting information, discovering that objects vary in shape, size, hardness, warmth, wetness and flavour. However, the act of grasping is also inform-ative and the brain simultaneously receives sensations of move-ment, touching, seeing and, sometimes hearing, tasting or smelling as well. Gradually some things come to be sucked, banged, twisted and so on: the baby brings together the different pieces of infor-mation, integrating them into one behaviour pattern. Thus the earliest of the schemata are born, and babies begin to form an image of the reality they experience. They also begin to demon-strate preferences.

In Chapter 2 reference was made to research into the develop-ment of Down's syndrome babies, which showed how long it took them to lose reflex actions. It was observed that psychological development was similarly retarded. Handicapped babies may make a late start in co-ordinated actions, and simple discrimin-ations, but without them they cannot acquire knowledge of the world they live in. They must experience, and so discover, that things can be made to move, or not; that they can be heavy or light; hard or soft; silent or noisy and so on. It is therefore import-ant that the opportunities for learning are present when the child can use them. Unfortunately, it is not always easy "to catch the moment as it flies" for development may be uneven. One of the teacher's tasks is to identify the gaps in attainment and knowledge as a prelude to filling them. This involves, among other things, ensuring that children have a variety of each kind of activity, so that sensory inputs can be integrated in all possible combinations.

This is all rather speculative, and it may be asked what evidence there is for the internalization of experience. There is certainly no way of opening up brains and seeing the schemata in them. However, there is some evidence to give credence to the theory. Babies who made a rattle swing when it was hanging within reach were observed by Piaget to make similar pushing movements with their hands when it was out of reach. This suggested that these babies knew the rattle as a thing to be swung by pushing. The fact that their abortive pushing movements were made indi-cates an incomplete internalization: the time will come when they will know the swinging potentiality without needing to move their hands.[2]

In this connection I have noticed that when confronted with odd objects in television quiz programmes, the participants often purse their lips and make little twitching movements. They also keep turning the object in a random fashion. When put into a situation of ignorance they revert to childish behaviours. Similarly, slow learning children, even in secondary schools, often put things to their mouths when they do not know what they are — understandably under the circumstances.

Feedback, the process by which the result of the child's actions modifies ongoing and subsequent behaviour, is an important feature of integration. Suppose that children are learning to colour in a shape: some may grasp the crayon so tightly that they can only make stabbing movements with it, and others so loosely that it wobbles about. As a result of kinaesthetic feedback (a report to the brain on the state of the muscles) loosening or tightening will correct the error, until a balance is struck. Then, when colouring, some strokes may not reach the outline and others go beyond it. In this case the feedback is visual: the eyes see and the hands get the message. If you can recall gripping the steering wheel when first learning to drive, and over-steering, you will understand the problem. Many adjustments have to be made before the performance is perfected.

Since the brain is kept constantly informed of the state of the muscles and bodily organs, and by the senses, all with their own feedback systems, the complexity of neural activity defies description. Nevertheless, the implication of this complexity is clear. Children need to repeat their actions time after time, and in a great variety of situations so that they have many opportunities of using their experience to improve their performance.

Imitation

It could be said that children who fill and empty sand buckets many times over are imitating themselves, but it is more usual to use the word when describing the way they match their behaviour to that of someone or something else that acts as a model. Before infants can imitate an action it has to be observed and attended to. They have to follow a moving object with their eyes (and sometimes with their heads) to see the sequence of movements. Imitating is a very large step forward. It enables them to attribute some events to their own behaviour and some to the behaviour of others. This helps them to consolidate the body-image.

Some of the achievements of young babies come about by their being taught to mimic by guiding the hands. Waving goodbye, and clapping "pat-a-cake" are very common. In both cases the sequence of movements is very simple, to and fro and up and down, and it does not matter if fro and to and down and up are substituted. Nevertheless, unless children can perform such an action at will, they will find it hard, if not impossible, to bring a spoon to their mouths, especially as feeding also involves getting food into the bowl of the spoon, opening the mouth at the right time, and taking the food off the bowl. This underlines the need to prompt the child to imitate, using bricks, beads, rods, balls and household articles, and larger pieces of equipment that can be pushed to encourage walking.

In general (but not inevitably) mentally handicapped babies are slow to sit up, creep, crawl, stand and walk, and also to play with the usual range of toys. They are especially slow at initiating new behaviours. It is therefore necessary for someone else to provide stimulation in a steady progression, by showing the child what a more alert baby might notice independently. Some of the most enjoyable and most educative playthings are very simple: wooden spoons and saucepan lids (with rolled edges) are favourites and encourage the co-ordination of both hands, banging and listening. The fact that the child is 3-years-old, or older, should not dissuade parents from showing their children how to learn these useful ways of playing. Later on, in play-group, nursery school or reception class, children pick up ideas from each other, though this may need organizing, and sustaining by adults.

Most infant and special schools have Wendy houses, shops, prams, toy cars and so on, and these encourage deferred imitation. Mentally handicapped children need the adults to be involved in their play, and it is important that they should be, for this type of fantasy is an introduction to symbolic thought. The pebbles on the doll's house plate symbolize food, for example. However, when children imitate they do not always understand the point of the exercise. They may use a toy brush and pan to mimic mother's actions when she beats an egg, and later on to sweep up crumbs in the Wendy house, but then walk away with the pan dangling. It will be considerably later that the brush and pan will be related to domestic hygiene.

Another form of deferred imitation comes in action songs such as "This is the way we wash our hands". These have the great advantage that they can be made more or less difficult. With older children they can become guessing games, one child performing an action and the others naming it. This makes explicit what may otherwise remain rather hazy. Good teachers get the most out of these traditional games. "Simon says" is another example. It can fulfil a number of purposes. With able children it is a way of enhancing alertness: with immature youngsters it can be kept to imitation and used to reinforce body awareness. When children can mime "This is the way we stamp our feet" the teacher can introduce "Simon says, Stamp your feet". Recalling the action without the model is a great advance on mimicry.

Imagery

The recall of objects or events, as though they were present in the environment is known as imagery. This is different from imagination in that imagery is related to what has been experienced, whereas imagination is about what could be, or could have been. However, imagery has the flavour of imagination for it includes using a shoebox as a bed, or a bath or even as a bus, though shoeboxes are not mobile in reality. These are very important signs to watch out for, because they herald the approach of communicative exchanges, as Piaget calls them.

The concepts of imagery and schemata are closely related, since imagery produces the behaviour on which assumptions about schemata are based. This is not just an academic point. Schemata result from interactions between the child and the environment: imagery, likewise, is constrained by the consequences of these interactions. This, as we shall see when discussing concept formation, is crucial. What has not "gone in" cannot "come out".

IMITATIVE PRACTICES

In school many planned activities involve some form of imitation, and, at home, in a less deliberate way, children engage in comparable occupations. One of these is matching. When children are asked to put bricks in one box and beads in another they employ an imitative technique, the one in which the least amount of decision-making is required. On other occasions they may be asked to separate large and small bricks. Here the task is more specific: they have to take one attribute into account ignoring others, such as colour. If there are only two sizes the task is much easier than if they have to decide on the dividing line.

When more than two groups are to be formed the task is called sorting, but the principle is the same. Having decided on the criterion, say colour, the child has to match reds, blues, greens and so on. Eventually two or more criteria are employed concurrently: tall boy, short boy, tall girl, short girl or tall dark boy, tall fair boy and so on. The materials which can be used for practice can include real-life activities. At home cups are normally put with cups, saucers with saucers, and people who live in an ordinarily tidy home know where to put things and where to find them. When children have learned in school how to match and sort, and how to apply these skills to classroom organization, parents can help them to apply the same methods, and thus make them more generally useful.

On returning from shopping, for example, children can help put away, at first just separating out things for the refrigerator, for the vegetable rack, for cleaning and so on. Later on they can differentiate tins of soup, fruit, fish and meat and small and large tins of each of them. If they can do this they can be asked to fetch father's slippers, or a small tin of tomatoes. It is, undoubtedly, often quicker and easier for teachers and parents to do these things themselves, but in the long run it is better for the child to learn to be independent. This contributes to his feeling of security.

Associated with such activities is language development, which itself includes elements of imitation, for children have to learn to match the sounds they make to those they hear, and words to objects or events. The process is similar when children learn a sign language, and to read and write.

The relationship of symbolic play to communication has already been given a brief mention. One problem with mentally handicapped children is that their slowly developing awareness of their own identity is paralleled by retardation in play. Intervention is therefore called for. This means that the child has to be encouraged, by being given a model to copy and by being praised for copying it.

In school, if children already understand some words, whether they say them or not, a form of bingo can be played. The teacher calls out the name of the object or action portrayed on a card, and the children holding a matching picture claim it. There is no need to play this game competitively. Similarly, picture dominoes is a matching game; it can be played by putting identical pictures together, or different pictures of the same kind of object, such as a kitchen chair and an armchair. The latter version is a classifying task, an advance on the simple matching of the former.[3]

When the child's fine-motor control is sufficiently advanced tracing and copying can begin. At first chubby crayons and pencils or felt-pens with fine points are best, since if the mimicry is to be effective the traced or copied version should be instantly recognizable. Boldness is helpful. One of the great advantages of tracing, copying and drawing (the last an example of deferred imitation) is that the product is there to be seen and discussed. As in other learning experiences children need to take many little steps many times, gradually making their performance more nearly match the model. It is a pity that most commercially produced colouring and tracing books are quite unsuitable for beginners, so parents may need to confer with their child's teacher before buying materials to use at home.

Comparing and Contrasting

When children compare objects and events and find them to be alike in certain ways, or contrast them to find the differences between them, they are making decisions which ultimately enable them to classify phenomena. This is a process without which it would be very difficult indeed to cope with new experiences or to categorize unfamiliar objects. The first step is to recognize whether and in which ways the similarities and differences recur. This is discrimination, an outcome of attention. The second is to organize on the basis of the discrimination. This is classification, or categorization.

Categorization can proceed in different directions. Dogs and cats, not always differentiated accurately by children, can form sub-groups according to breed, geographical distribution and so on, or alternatively can be included in larger groups, carnivores, mammals, domestic pets, and so on. These ways of classifying, which only emerge with advancing years, develop out of the many sorting tasks initiated by parents, teachers and the children themselves. Every time a child helps with tidying up classification is practised, unless, of course, tidying means throwing everything into a toy-box. Children take time to learn to classify in an adult manner. They first put items together in a random fashion, and need to be prompted to make decisions based on colour, size, shape, use, material, texture, smell and so on, moving very gradually from matching to sorting tasks.

Comparing and Contrasting Quantities

There is a very important difference between describing the items which are put together to make a group or set, and naming the number of items in the set. The members may be dogs, chairs and so on, or miscellaneous items, and their number may be, say, five. All groups of five have "fiveness" in common. Put together with a group of three a new group of eight will be formed, irrespective of whatever items form the groups.

Recognizing that a set of items has a numerical attribute is the basis of counting, and it is generally agreed that children should learn to count if they can. What is entailed in counting is, nevertheless, not always appreciated. The process involves comparing and contrasting quantities, and learning the word which describes the number of the group.

In the first place it is the ability to match two groups by what is known as one-to-one correspondence. If two groups have equal numbers of members then pairing one from each of the groups leaves none unmatched. This establishes the concept of equality, or, if there is a remainder, of inequality, for the groups are seen to be the same or different. An extension of this is to identify which group has more (is bigger) or less (is smaller) and then how many more or less. It is at this stage that a child must be able to give the right number names to the groups, and to the differences between them.

This is quite difficult. When children point to the rabbits in a picture saying "One, two, three, four, five" they are, in fact, pointing to one rabbit at a time, and are not obviously forming successive groups of one to five. When they count the stairs as they climb them there is no way that the stairs can be seen to be sets of increasing size. What would be more accurate, but certainly no easier, would be to say, "First, second, third, fourth and fifth" (ordinal numbers) and then to infer that the number of steps climbed must be five (cardinal number). The more one looks at what underlies counting the more pitfalls one finds. Yet children, including some with severe learning difficulties, do learn to count, albeit with varying degrees of understanding. What we need to ensure is the maximum possible comprehension, for unless the children know what is meant by each number name their counting will be unreliable, and of little value.

Some experiences occur daily. Getting dressed is one, and since children have two arms, legs, hands, feet, eyes and ears there are many opportunities for establishing the concept of two. Socks, shoes, sleeves and gloves come in pairs and can be counted as they are put on. In this way the number name is matched to the action. In developing the number system it is important that counting is not divorced from action and that written number is not introduced prematurely. This does not mean that children should not memorize the numbers in sequence nor learn to write them, but rather that their counting by rote should not greatly outstrip their ability to count objects, if at all.

Counting errors can occur because items are omitted or included more than once. For this reason counting objects is preferred to counting pictures on a page, for they can be physically shifted with the result that, as the group is repositioned, the cardinal number is used correctly. When the third brick is moved a group of three is made and "three" is said. (In this context a picture card is an object since it can be moved.) Usually the objects are identical at first, but it is necessary to establish that numerically a cat, dog and horse is the same as a kettle, frying pan and colander. Flannel board (marketed as Fuzzy Felt) and felt cut-outs are very useful for matching groups, and for forming groups either larger or smaller than the model. Such activities lead to considerable flexibility in counting, and are an important part of the number curriculum. Unfortunately, there is little to show at this stage and parents may feel dissatisfied because they have no tangible evidence of their child's progress. This puts teachers under pressure, especially in schools for children with moderate learning difficulties.

The reality is that what goes on in the head is what matters, and parents who are uneasy should feel free to discuss this with the staff. They can also observe progress for themselves in simple ways, watching for the ability to put the right number of plates on the table (an application of one-to-one correspondence, or two-to-one if side plates are used). When the child can move from picture to number dominoes, or can play simple number track games, parents can see for themselves the foundations that have been laid.

Sometimes even the simplest of board games present difficulties because the principles of taking turns and moving the counter according to the way the die falls are not understood. If this is so a home-made game may help to overcome this difficulty.[4]

Order and Arrangement

When children can discriminate and classify they can see relationships between objects which vary regularly or irregularly. The natural number system itself can be considered as a series of groups with a regular difference of one. But there are other series: children can arrange objects according, among other things, to length, height, overall size, distance or weight, the last being the most difficult. At first they learn descriptive words: long, big, heavy and so on, and then to compare two objects: a car can be big, but smaller than a truck. The next stage is to order three or more objects. Toys such as Russian dolls present opportunities of ordering items.

The ability to order is tied up with the concept of conservation, by which is implied that numbers and measures are not altered by changing their arrangement. Children who learn slowly have such a struggle to master the foundations of mathematics that they may be given only one arrangement of number, the most usual being the domino pattern. This, however, is an obstacle to forming the concept of conservation, and is another argument for a slow and thorough start, with an emphasis on ringing the changes. Children must be able to count objects however they are presented.

Understanding spatial arrangement comes with experiences of putting things into, taking them out of, placing them on, under, behind, in front of other things, and is enhanced by appropriate language, either hearing or using it, or both. Such language expresses the positional relationship between two objects. Quantitative and temporal expressions, such as "first", "more than", or "after tea" are also relational. It must be just as hard for some children to master the variety of everyday relationships as it is for many of us to understand relativity. Children who cannot walk or who have manipulative disabilities are especially at a disadvantage, for it is, for example, experiences such as trying to push a pram through a narrow space that drive home the concept of width.

AUTOMATIC RESPONSES

The result of repeatedly matching, sorting, ordering and arranging objects is so to master them that responses will be automatically evoked. It has been said that the more we can do without thinking, the more we can think. Tasks that necessitate stopping to consider or to make decisions or to carry out intentions generally include an automatic element, or sequence of elements. The more easily these automations are evoked the more freedom the child has to make decisions.

The automatic-sequential element of spoken language is particularly important, for in order to converse sounds must be articulated in the right order to make words, and words follow each other to convey the message, and they must do so spontaneously. If there is a pause it should be to wonder what to say, not how to make the right noises. This implies a store of speaking skills on which to draw — not the only consideration, but a fundamental one without which utterances cannot develop. The child's utterances may be simple, only one, two or three words, but even so speech organs have to be used delicately and precisely for the message to be conveyed to the listener. As everyone knows from experience, young children do not always succeed in making themselves understood by strangers in their early attempts at conversation. Practice, feedback and encouragement are all needed to enable them to produce a steady flow of intelligible sounds, a skill which is discussed in Chapter 8. In this context what is being emphasized is that, just as reaching and grasping are fundamental to many physical activities, articulating sounds is basic to speech and must occur just as automatically and in proper sequence. The fact that most children learn to talk without special help should not minimize the achievement. Instead, the complexity of the task indicates how important it is that mentally handicapped children should be encouraged to keep on practising making sounds, babbling and so on, for it is this which lays the essential foundations of speech. If adults imitate the child's prattle in a responding tone of voice, so that a conversational exchange takes place, not only are speech sounds encouraged, but the essentially communicative aspects of language are emphasized.

However, speech is not the only way of communicating. The idiosyncratic means which are used, the gestures and so on, also have an underpinning of automatic-sequential behaviour, which, like sound blending and grammar, operate below the level of consciousness. These can be the foundations of a signing system, which is more flexible than gesture, and more susceptible to generalization. The first step is to bring to a conscious level the means to be used, through the processes already discussed — imitation, matching and ordering. Then, by repeated and rewarded practice, their use becomes unconscious.[5]

Evoked behaviour does not necessarily imply comprehension. There was a time when it was not unusual for mentally handicapped children to approach every visitor to the classroom asking, "What's your name?" This, in my experience, seldom happens now, and is not to be regretted for when answered the question was generally repeated, parrot-fashion, and a reply did not seem to be informative. The word "tuffet" can be evoked by saying, "Little Miss Muffet sat on a ———" but it is doubtful if this makes sense to the child. This does not mean that evocation should always be eschewed. One cannot be sure for example that children can anticipate the consequences of dangerous practices, and will avoid them for that reason. In these matters evoked behaviour may be as crucial for children as it is for motorists to stop at red traffic lights.

ANTICIPATION AND PREDICTION

Completing a sentence such as, "Mother is going to the shop to buy some —" is not at all the same thing as filling gaps in a nursery rhyme. The former requires knowledge of what is possible. It permits a large range of answers that depend on past experience or inference. The child may have been with mother on many occasions when bread was bought, but not jigsaws. Nevertheless, the inference could be made that mother could buy some jigsaws, and either answer would meet the requirements of the task. It is the ability to associate past and present events that allows the child to predict future ones.

This opens up a whole range of possibilities. It enables the child to look forward, to make plans and to see, in advance, the consequences of present behaviour. Children who can anticipate outcomes are not operating without some understanding. They are able to take responsibility, limited though it may be. They can respond intelligently to, "It's raining. What coat will you put on today?" for they can bring into focus the mental image of getting wet. Or they can choose sensibly between even and uneven surfaces when placing a cup of tea, or the amount of peas to help themselves to and so on, according to whatever has been the content of their previous experiences.

What unites imitation, evocation, automatic-sequential behaviour and prediction is that they are all expressions of interactions between the child and the real world of objects and events. They arise directly from the child's experiences, not from what has been merely told or shown, but what has been done. They become possible because repetition has resulted in their being so habitual that they only have to be sparked off to be followed through without awareness of the steps in the process. This is what Professor Meredith implied when he spoke of "well-trodden pathways." It is only on unfamiliar territory that the travellers have to pay attention to the route. On the other hand, when the route is familiar, they can more easily register unexpected hazards and take evasive action promptly enough to keep out of trouble.

INTEGRATION AND PERCEPTION

When children know that the animal they see is a cat and instantly recognize it as one, or know how to put their socks on, they are demonstrating that a number of pieces of information have come together to form an integrated whole. Their experiences of cats may include their size, shape, colour, smell, furriness, style of movement, scratchiness, meowing and so on. Similarly, their experience of putting socks on may include not only their appearance and feel, but also reaching for and grasping them, directing them to their feet, tensing and relaxing muscles in feet, ankles and legs, and so on. Thus, in both cases, selections of different sensory inputs come together as one. First, they have to notice the cat or the socks and then to make sense of what is noticed by integrating the sensations and by relating them to similar experiences (see Figure 4.1).

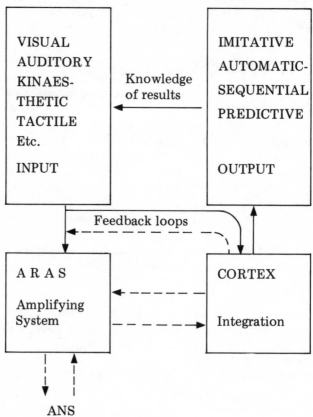

Figure 4.1   A simple model of learning at the integration level of organization

This making sense of what is noticed is sometimes called perception, which could be said to be the subject matter of this chapter. But perception is a tricky word, for it carries with it preconceptions which may just as readily lead to misunderstanding as to understanding. Besides that, in the field of educational handicap, it has come to have special connotations related to particular methods of remediation. For these reasons, the words information and knowledge have been used where other writers (not necessarily without justification) would have written about perceiving.

Perceptual Handicaps

Children who have specific difficulties in coping with sensory information (and they may or may not be handicapped in other ways) are sometimes said to have visual-perceptual, auditory-perceptual or perceptual-motor disabiltiies. Such a diagnosis does not mean that they have impaired sight or vision, nor that they are physically handicapped. They do, however, find that using their eyes or ears to make sense of their environment is not straight-forward, or they may be noticeably clumsy and find that imitating gestures is extremely difficult.

One problem which may confront them is that of isolating from a complicated background the particular feature they need. This is an attentional-perceptual difficulty: in figure-ground tasks the feedback system may become overloaded, because of the excessive amount of input from which what is sought cannot be found. This situation can be compared with an adult's when trying to sort out the constituent flavours of an unfamiliar dish. When told that lemon juice has been missed it is immediately recognized. If told that coriander is present it might be a different matter: it would depend on previous experience.

Children who have similar difficulties with sight, hearing or movement need plenty of practice with familiar input and reduced demand, especially until they realize what it is they are supposed to be doing. The value of many learning aids lies, to a very great extent, on the way they clarify the purpose of the task.

In some ways it is misleading to use the expression 'perceptual handicap', for the suggestion is that the child has something (comparable to extra ribs) when we should generally be thinking in terms of an ability a child has not developed. "Generally" because damage to the brain, which a child might rightly be said to have, may make the development of certain abilities very difficult or even impossible. Nevertheless, there is no cut-off point separating children with and without perceptual difficulties, nor is there a dividing line which makes some behaviour perceptual and some representational (see Chapter 6). Cortical activity is involved in all behaviour. What characterizes integration is that actions (in the broadest sense) arise out of direct involvement with the real world, and are repeated until they can occur without awareness. If this is so the child can be said to know something, or to know how to do something. This is knowledge that brings foresight.

NOTES AND REFERENCES

1. MEREDITH, P. (1970) *Learning, Remembering and Knowing*, London, English Universities Press.
2. PIAGET, J. (1970) "Piaget's theory" in P.H. MUSSEN (ed.) *Carmichael's Manual of Child Psychology*, Vol. I, 3rd edition. New York, John Wiley.
3. The catalogue *Learning Development Aids* lists materials designed in the UK especially for these purposes. The sister company Living and Learning, supplies materials from overseas. Both are available from Duke St., Wisbech, Cambs. PE13 2AE. Comparable aids are listed by Beckley-Cardy, P.O. Box 469, New Berlin, Wisconsin, USA 53151.
4. This game is useful for children who cannot quite manage published board games.

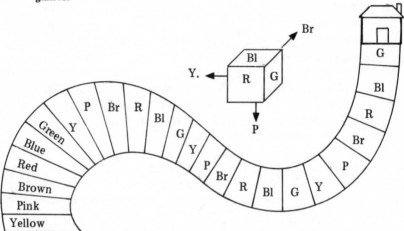

Draw "The Way Home" with repeated sequences of six colours. Make a die to match the colours, one colour to each face; covered foam, card or a cut-down covered milk carton can be used. Each player has a counter or a miniature person or car to move. Players throw the die turn by turn moving the counter onto the square of the colour they have thrown. No counting is involved. Have only two players at first, one adult and one child, and progress from there. Variations can be invented: for example, rebuses can be used, but avoid number in any form.

5. Signing systems are discussed in:

DIECH, R.F. and HODGES, P.U. (1977) *Language Without Speech*, London, Souvenir Press.

KIERNAN, C. *et al.* (1978) *Starting Off*, London, Souvenir Press.

TEBBS, T. (ed.) (1978) *Ways and Means* Basingstoke, Globe Educational.

KIERNAN, C. *et al.* (1979) "Signs and symbols — who uses what?" in *Special Education: Forward Trends*, Vol. 6, No. 4.

FRISTOE, M. and LLOYD, L.L. (1979) "Non-speech communication" in N. ELLIS (ed.) *Handbook of Mental Deficiency*, 2nd edition. New York, John Wiley.

5

LEARNING AND MEMORY

"... and still the wonder grew
That one small head could carry all he knew"   Oliver Goldsmith

This chapter is organized differently from those in the rest of this book. First there is an introduction to contemporary approaches to the study of memory. This is because of the amount of recent research and discussions of the controversial implications of experimental findings. In order to clarify issues these have produced a far from illuminating proliferation of terminology and acronyms from which a limited number has been abstracted for the purpose of this brief overview. Second, research into developmental aspects of memory will be recounted, and third, these will be applied, tentatively, to the problem of improving the memory of handicapped children and young people.

It is interesting that we seldom draw attention to the number and varieties of things we remember but quite often to our shocking memory for names, or other lapses. Yet an essential element of learning and knowing is our ability to use, after an interval of time, what has been previously acquired — no mean achievement. It is through memory and imagination that, in the words of Sir Frederic Bartlett, "we find the most complete release from the narrowness of time and place".[1]

This important attribute, memory, is not a possession, a thing which a person either has or has not, but the name given to the processes that are used to register, retain and retrieve our experiences. These processes vary from person to person, from occasion to occasion and from time to time. Thus some people remember most easily what they have seen, and others what they have heard; some happenings are easily recalled while others remain hazy. Memory also changes as years come and go. Why these should be so is only partially understood. Nevertheless, evidence is accumulating and, as a consequence, fresh hypotheses are being explored.

STAGES OF MEMORY

Although the one word "memory" is used, psychologists have long since differentiated between what is only temporarily "held in the mind" and what is of indefinite duration, which they now sometimes refer to as primary and secondary memory (PM and SM). Some prefer a three-stage storage system of sensory memory, PM and SM. Sensory memory, they suggest, is linked to attention. In this stage, sensory input enters the appropriate store, which is able to deal with a large amount of information, but only for a very brief time, usually only a fraction of a second. The arguments for and against storage theories do not, at first sight, appear to be relevant to education. However, the discussions express ideas about how the brain holds knowledge and understanding for future use, which is surely relevant.

The very use of words like "hold" and "store" suggests some sort of spatial system, with a place for every memory and every memory in its place, a controversial matter. Another approach is to emphasize the processing nature of memory by referring to active and passive storage instead of short and long-term stores. The contributions made by physiologists fit the active—passive model. They describe how new information is encoded in spatial and temporal patterns of electrochemical signals travelling towards and in the brain, which is reached in thousandths of a second. In other words, sensations reach the brain, almost instantaneously, by way of the nervous system, in a coded form, rather like microelectronics and quite unlike the way pictures are recorded on films. Impulses are then actively held in channels of limited capacity, PM, or passively stored in large capacity, SM. There are three explanations for the short duration of input in PM: fading or displacement or both. Impulses may die away and, or, they may be pushed out by the impulses which succeed them. Whichever is the case, it is apparent that there must be some mechanism or mechanisms to prevent bottlenecks. The evidence is that information decays or is displaced in about half a minute, unless it is kept active. A memory system which did not include such forgetting would be highly inefficient, for it would require unlimited storage capacity and would present enormous retrieval problems. Children do not need to remember, for ever, all the cars that pass them on their way to school. On the contrary, they need to forget them.

However, they may need to remember the number of the bus that takes them there and gets them home, an item of information that goes into SM or passive storage. There is evidence to show that this cannot be the same as active storage. For example, when coma interferes with electrochemical transmission, so that no primary processes are possible, SM is not affected and remains intact. This suggests that there must be structural or chemical modifications of the nervous system, or both, to enable memories to be retained. It is thought that these structural and chemical changes occur at the synapses, the narrow gaps along the nerve pathways, which thicken with use to form synaptic knobs.[2]

While memories remain in passive storage they do not affect thinking or behaviour. To do this they must become active again, through the processes of retrieval: recognition and recall. It has been shown that the neural activity that occurs during acquisition is reactivated when the information is recalled. This points to interaction between PM and SM, both at registration and retrieval stages. It is also possible that unless the systems interact from time to time during the retention stage, memories fade, or are displaced or become so overlaid that they are beyond recall. Although the fluid state between PM and SM is fully acknowledged, research tends to concentrate on short-term processes, which are more readily controlled than long-term retention, though never without some complications. The task can be to name an array of objects that have been presented for a specified time, as in Kim's game; or to repeat a sentence or string of digits; or to recall an arrangement of patterned tiles. Subjects can be given lists of words or pictures to learn and asked which succeeded which (a serial learning task), or pairs of words or pictures and asked to remember one when given the other (paired-associate learning). Other tasks include recalling prose passages of various lengths. Sometimes recognition instead of recall is demanded. The mode of presentation, and the interval between presentation and recall, are two of a number of possible variables. Such a variety of methods and materials has produced many pieces of patchwork, unfortunately not all matching each other, some clashing and, inevitably, an unfinished quilt.

Another reason for exploring primary memory is the assumption that unless the short-term mechanisms are activated there is

no possibility of long-term retention. The memories of the coma-
tose patient may not be reduced: they can in no way be increased.
Thus, understanding the first steps in laying down a store of
memories is a logical starting point.

Nevertheless, remembering and forgetting, in the more
general long-term sense, are of great concern in everyday life. It is
thought that adults may recall as many as 10,000 items daily. So
far, such complexity has frustrated psychologists, and no model of
SM has yet been devised to embrace all the possible contingencies.

Primary Memory

It has already been shown that PM and SM have different characteristics. PM has limited capacity with rapid forgetting, and with
no permanent record, either psychologically (in behaviour) or
physiologically (in the nervous system itself). Further differences
are the ease, speed and exactness of recalling the items that are
not forgotten. It is probable that verbal items are held in PM in
terms of sounds, not meanings.

The rate of presentation of items affects the outcome. For
example, at fast rates auditory presentation is superior to visual
presentation while slowing the rate of presentation produces the
opposite effect. There is also a difference in outcome if visual
items are presented as an array, and not one by one.

If all that is required in verbal tasks is "play-back", the
actual words that are presented do not materially affect the
number recalled (about four words in a strictly-controlled experiment). The objective when researching PM is to eliminate or
control the strategies that might be employed to overcome the
inherent limitations of the short-term process.

Convenience, as well as intrinsic interest, is responsible for
concentration on verbal and pictorial items, but memory for tones,
movement and touch have also been investigated with similar
results. In all cases the capacity of PM has been shown to be
limited and forgetting very rapid. However, there is a strategy for
increasing the length of time that information is held in PM. This
strategy is rehearsal. If the interval between presentation and recall
is left blank, information can be repeated "in the head" (or out
loud, in the way one mutters a telephone number) and its life
prolonged. This important process of rehearsal or recirculation
also provides a means whereby material can be transferred to
passive storage. This will depend on purpose and the intention to
remember, and whether it is possible to integrate new material
into the existing structures of SM.

It is possible to prevent rehearsal during an experiment. The subject can, for example, be required to carry out an activity such as counting backwards from twenty as soon as the information to be remembered has been presented. Such a task considerably interferes with the amount recalled.

Secondary Memory

Whereas PM has to be able to cope with immediate input in the form in which it is presented, SM has to provide means of using the acquired skills of a lifetime, especially, but not only, language skills. It is also through SM that previous experiences can be recalled. The first is known as semantic memory because of its relationship to meaning and intention, and the second as episodic memory. Memory for movement is also enduring and activities such as riding a bicycle can be resumed after long intervals.

Semantic memory is not concerned with the circumstances that surrounded acquisition. The words or the manual skills we need to meet our purposes usually come to us instantly, without consciousness of searching the memory and without unnecessary associations. When the word "able" is used to mean "possible" the alternatives, "powerful, intelligent, useful, skilful, -bodied, and -seaman" are not evoked. The way words or bicycle riding are stored, regardless of the circumstances of storage, makes for an economical and highly efficient system.

On the other hand episodes are stored, it is thought, on the basis of the time, place and circumstances of their occurence. To retrieve these is a conscious process (though memories may flood back unexpectedly) requiring the support of semantic memory, and time for probing and restoring associations. It is a common ploy when something cannot be found to recall circumstantial detail — who was last seen with it, where, when and so on.

Episodes, by definition, are incidents viewed as separate occurences; they include films, books, TV programmes and so on. It is reasonable to expect episodes to make sense: what sometimes reinforces registration, and subsequently retrieval, is a disparity between what is observed and what is expected. The important point is that whereas many details may be recalled from, for example, the single reading of a novel it may take many repetitions to remember a telephone number or a postal code. It is more rewarding, presumably, to make an effort after the meaning of a TV play than a postal code. However, the effort may not lead to accuracy, for interpretation is influenced by previous experience by both additions and subtractions. The greater the interval between registration and recall, the more likely it is that memory will be distorted.

CONTROL PROCESSES

Rehearsal is not the only strategy that can be used to enhance remembering. Many means are used, from tying knots in handkerchiefs to remembering that PIECES OF STRING tie up the curriculum (Physical, Intellectual, Educational, Cultural, Emotional, Social factors and Short Term Realizable INteresting Goals).* These, and other strategies, are under voluntary control and are, in principle, amenable to training. Generally, grouping material to be remembered is productive. When going over what is required to cook a meal the recipe may list rice, steak, onions, mushrooms, salt, pepper, cream, lemon and parsley. Rice, salt and pepper can be ignored because they are in stock (and it is important to know what can be forgotten, for this reduces the load) and onions, mushrooms, lemon and parsley regrouped. This decreases the chance of overlooking one, for, among other things, the fact that there are four items will be stored. If necessary the memory can be searched for the missing one, or the shop scanned to prompt recognition. Recalling an image of beef Stroganoff will help to recall parsley, but not lemon, for it is included only to make the cream sour. Organization of material to be remembered, with category names (butcher's, greengrocer's, dairy) aids recall.

Reducing the load on memory makes some retrieval easier. If the fact that dogs bark and so on is stored in the memory it is only necessary to store "A terrier is a dog" to recall doggy attributes. They do not need to be stored for every individual dog or breed. This is an advantage of classification.

Sometimes, however, it is better to add to the information one wishes to retain. In everyday life names and faces present a very common paired-associate task. The association between the two is quite arbitrary and needs elaborating into a short word-portrait, and probably rehearsal too. The point of elaboration is to increase routes to the required end. "I remember the face but not the name" is frequently heard. Recognition, in general, is easier than recall, if only because there are only two choices for the former (you either can or you cannot) but many for the latter.

*I am indebted to Peter W. Young for this mnemonic.

Besides that, the presence of the face acts as a prompt, and prompting aids recall. Figure 5.1, a model of memory processes, indicates, very simply, how material is kept circulating in order to retain it and to retrieve it.

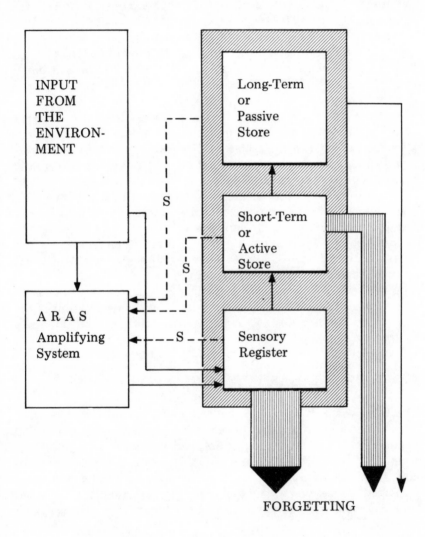

Figure 5.1 A model of memory processes The strategies of rehearsing, organizing and elaborating are shown by the feedback loops - -S- -. Most input is lost from the sensory register

Metamemory

Awareness of one's own memory, and what strategies are available and appropriate to specific tasks, has a long history but has only had a title since 1977. This field of study, which includes "Tip of the tongue" and "Feeling of knowing" phenomena is now called Metamemory. Bringing together and organizing work in this field is potentially a most important contribution to improving memory, for it deals with the aspects that are susceptible to training. It is possible that the complexity of modern life on one hand, and the efficiency of microprocessing on the other, has stimulated this interest.

A metamemorial ability that has not yet been mentioned is "Feeling of not-knowing". This seemingly trivial experience is of immense theoretical importance. If we knew how the brain was able to identify at great speed what has not been stored we would know a great deal more than we do about storage. However, children who have been accustomed to failure in school are over-ready to say, "Don't know". One often meets this when administering an individual test, and finds that with prompting and encouragement the answer is forthcoming. Sometimes this is a problem of motivation, not of memory, though the two interact to strengthen or weaken each other.

There is much more to the study of memory than has been touched on. What has been selected leads to a consideration of the developmental aspects of memory in children and mentally retarded young people.

DEVELOPMENTAL ASPECTS OF MEMORY

The three main ways of improving memory in adults are rehearsal, which prevents information from being lost from PM; organizing into categories when storing in SM; and using the same categories when recalling as when storing and elaborating. It is possible to do any of these consciously and deliberately. An interesting and important question is whether children and mentally retarded young people can use these strategies, and if they can use them whether they do so.

The way that even very young babies exercise choice, express recognition and repeat pleasurable activities suggests that memory functions from birth, and that from the earliest weeks the active mind of the child is involved in what is being stored, unconsciously, and without any intention to remember. By the third year the rapid learning of vocabulary is another indication that a long-term store of semantic memory is being accumulated. In children with severe learning difficulties these indications come more slowly.

Many children appear to be good at remembering, and to be very quick at retrieval. If something is mislaid at home it is often a young child who will know immediately where to find it. Nevertheless, the evidence that young children build up their long-term store of memories neither supports nor contradicts a case for developmental changes in the capacity of primary memory or metamemory.

Memory in Young Children

Some of the earliest work on memory in children was carried out by an American, John Flavell, in the late 1960s. He and his colleagues showed three groups of twenty children, aged 5, 7 and 10 years, sets of seven pictures and pointed to three of them. The children, who were tested individually, were wearing space helmets with a visor that could be pulled down for fifteen seconds. When it was lifted the children had to point to the same three pictures. The results showed that this ability improved with age, and close observation showed that whereas only two of the 5-year-olds showed by lip-movements that they were rehearsing, seventeen of the 10-year-olds spontaneously recirculated the items. The lip-movements at all ages were correlated with good retrieval.[3]

When this finding was followed up by other researchers it was found that young children could rehearse, if they were shown how to. When they did so the amount that they recalled equalled that of the children who rehearsed without instruction. However, when the advice to whisper the names of the pictures was no longer given the children stopped whispering.

In the same way, when asked to remember an array of pictures older children regrouped them under category headings, and used their reorganization during recall. Young children adopted a haphazard approach unless shown how to rearrange the material in their heads. Again, the adoption of this strategy brought their performance up to the level of the older children, but again, when the advice was not given the technique was not used. Variations on the use of this strategy produced comparable results. Young children can employ coding or clustering strategies but do not do so unless urged, whereas older children need no additional encouragement. The change takes place round about 9 years.

Memory in Retarded Young People

The most thorough report of research in the UK into the memory processes of children and young people with severe learning difficulties is an account of work carried out by Peter Herriot, Josephine Green and Roy McConkey at the Hester Adrian Research Centre, University of Manchester. It is one of a number of *Studies in Mental Handicap.*[4]

Herriot and his associates chose approximately 550 subjects from special schools and adult training centres (sheltered workshops for the mentally handicapped) whose vocabulary ages ranged from 5 to 8 years, who were able to name articles such as chair, boat, clock and kettle and recall them. For any one experiment the subjects had similar chronological ages.

The main aim of the project was to discover whether the same processes could be inferred to account for the free recall performance of young mentally handicapped adults as are hypothesized to account for that of normals. Each of the twelve subtests was administered individually, all but one using the free-recall technique. Each experiment was carried out by one of the team members, aided by a colleague who managed the equipment. The material was visual — an array of pictures shown on a film slide. This allowed the young people to view haphazardly, or to group the items. Recall was immediate and subjects were prompted, if necessary, with questions such as, "Anything else?" It is evident from this description that many hours of close attention were devoted to this project.

There is more than enough evidence that the amount of material that is recognized or recalled within seconds of presentation increases with age and general ability. Retarded children, as a group, recall less well than ordinary children of the same age, and as well as younger children of the same general ability (expressed as a mental age). There are, however, differences within the groups as well as between them which are often overlooked. The question is: do the findings suggest defect or developmental delay?

Experiments using control groups of either the same chronological or mental age as the retarded children highlight the presence of a defect (by odious comparison). This can lead to the pessimistic conclusion that poor performance is inevitable. On the other hand if differences are found within groups there is some incentive to search for the conditions which produce the better performances, and encouragement to enhance the performances of the weaker children.

The Hester Adrian Research Centre Project

Before commencing their studies Herriot, Green and McConkey summarized previous research which showed that the amount that severely retarded people recalled, and the order in which items were recalled could be influenced by experimental intervention. This suggests that strategies are potentially available (as they were shown to be in young children) even when they are not used.

In the first experiment the subjects were children of school age. In this, forty-eight 12-year-olds, with an average vocabulary age of just over 5 years, were shown sets of six pictures on each of three successive days. One set was of three pairs of items (e.g., one pair might be a car and a train); the other two sets were of unrelated articles. The primary task was to see if this was a realistic task to follow up, by estimating the amount recalled from the related and the unrelated sets of pictures. The consistency between the scores in the three days was also established. A test which gives different results on different days cannot be relied on.

The findings, though open to interpretation, were encouraging, and have since been replicated. The differences between the scores that would be expected by chance and those that were actually observed were large enough to justify the conclusion that the children remembered items in pairs, although the presentation was random. Clustering also went with increases in the amount recalled.

By the end of the twelve investigations the team had detailed evidence that some retarded persons can use strategies to improve the amount they can recall in a memory task. When they were given category names at presentation and recall, or the opportunity to sort items into categories, the amount they recalled was increased. Subjects whose vocabulary age was 7 to 8 years were given only general instructions to organize ("Put together the things that go together") and this was found to be sufficient. Since then Green has added to the findings, and it is now thought that some adults with vocabulary ages of under 6 years can also respond to reminders to organize items.

Metamemory in Young and Retarded Children

Young children do not appear to be aware of how they remember. They cannot tell in advance what would be easy or difficult, or what strategies they could use to help them, for instance, to remember a telephone number until they had dialled it. When in fact they elaborate or reduce information they seem to do so without planning. They act as though memory comes naturally, which, of course, it does, and consequently make little deliberate effort to remember. As they grow older their awareness awakens, for they realize the advantage of intending to remember, and they know what strategies help them. They become increasingly able "to plan to use a plan".

The improvement in the performance of mentally handicapped young people when following instructions to group items suggests that they too are unaware of the strategies that are available to them. There is also evidence that even when strategies are available they do not know which to select. When no strategies can be used there is no difference in the performances of young children, retarded adolescents and college students. The tasks which have demonstrated this include recognizing whether a picture has been included in a long list of pictures presented one at a time; judging whether the length of a line is the same as one previously seen; and recalling when and where an item has been seen. Episodic memory in retarded children has also been shown to be comparable to that of non-retarded children, if the original learning has been the same.

The inference is that young people with severe learning difficulties need to learn what to concentrate on, how to use incidental information, to cluster, to elaborate on material, and to rehearse, and, most importantly, which to do and to realize that they are doing it. For a young person who has severe learning difficulties this is indeed a monumental task and may take many years.

TRAINING CHILDREN TO REMEMBER

Results from experiments can only direct attention to what happens under controlled, and often artificial, conditions. What actually happens in real life could be a different matter. It is, therefore, always necessary to be on the alert and ready to observe under what conditions, or in what way, children use their memories effectively.

The major problem appears to be in the short-term processes of primary memory. Children with sufficient language can generally give a reasonable account of a day's outing or a birthday party, and can remember their addresses and the names of their friends. It is tasks such as taking a message from one teacher to another that they find difficult. If any distraction is encountered *en route* they may not even remember that they are on an errand, let alone remember the message itself. If a pupil who has been withdrawn for individual work is sent back to the classroom with a request for another child, more often than not the teacher has to guess who is wanted. This is a serious weakness, for it indicates a breakdown that can affect learning at source. If children do not manage short-term retention their "working memory" is impaired and all acquisition is thereby endangered.

Practical suggestions can only be tentative, based on experience as well as research. In the first place I think that the staff of a school should together decide on their objectives and the general methods they intend to employ. This is as important a curricular decision as any other. Basically there are two things to learn: the plans themselves and how to execute them.

When a child is learning to take a message it is a good idea for teachers to collaborate beforehand, or to have a code, such as a book that can be carried to and fro, so that the messenger can be helpfully prompted if necessary. At first the message should be very short. "Thank you" would do. Then the details should be revised. "Where are you going?" "Who are you going to give that book to?" "What are you going to say?" It is evident that taking the simplest message makes considerable demands on the limited channel capacity of PM.

As children set out they should be told to remember to whisper, "Thank you" all the way. Both instructions should be given, to remember and to whisper, since the two-fold objective is to train children to be aware of memory and have the intention to use it. Later the instruction can be to whisper the message "in your head".

There are many changes that can be rung, and there must be very few schools where something of the sort is not done, but perhaps not as thoroughly, or consistently as necessary. Occasions arise when organizing the items to be remembered is part of a task. With older children this comes into many of the real-life skills they need to learn, such as shopping, home economics and craft. Again, it is being aware of the advantages of clustering that is important.

The incomplete evidence that is available suggests that most children with severe learning difficulties will not be ready to benefit from this kind of training until they are in their teens, and some not then. Prior to that they will be acquiring knowledge and skills without being aware of acquisition processes. However, they can be introduced to the idea of memory by playing simple memory games, and by learning in a way that emphasizes remembering. For example, the large and clear pictures in *Jim's People*[5] can be used. The children can be shown one, told to look, close their eyes, and on opening them say whether the picture has been changed. Interspersing such a task with advice using "memory vocabulary" is helpful.

Whether children with severe learning difficulties can learn to use their memories efficiently and independently is uncertain. The tendency of research until recently has been to look for what is wrong (the defect orientation) instead of seeking means to bring about improvement (the developmental orientation). We cannot, therefore, be sure that we are yet using the best possible ways of teaching children. What we do know, which is encouraging, is that when young people are interested in pop songs, or football, food or clothes they can remember quite a lot. If the potential is there the aim must be to release it.

NOTES AND REFERENCES

1. BARTLETT, F.C. (1932) *Remembering*, Cambridge University Press.

2. MILLER, R.R. (1978) "Some physiological aspects of memory", in M.M. GRUNEBERG and P. MORRIS (eds.) *Aspects of Memory*. This is dealt with in more detail in Chapter 6.

3. FLAVELL, J.H. (1970) "Developmental studies of mediated memory" in H.W. REESE and L.P. LIPSITT (eds.) *Advances in Child Development and Behaviour*, Vol. 5, New York, Academic Press.

4. HERRIOT, P., GREEN, J. and McCONKEY, R. (1973) *Organisation and Memory*, London, Methuen.

5. THOMAS, B., GASKIN, S. and HERRIOT, P. (1973) *Jim's People*, Wisbech, L.D.A. This is three boxed sets of pictures specially designed for use in language development programmes. They are large, clear and uncluttered.

6

SURPRISE WAYS

"The mind becomes what it does"   H. Overstreet

During the 1970s the Schools Council (a national body) set up a project on teaching language and communication to the mentally handicapped.[1] The project team worked in nineteen schools and surveyed the language skills of 1,381 mentally retarded children aged 2 to 19 years. In the course of their investigations they questioned the teachers and parents of the children about the intellectual or academic aims of education and received similar replies from both groups. "Teachers", they reported, "were not only anxious to foster the child's ability to learn but also to think critically and imaginatively and develop his ability to cope with and adapt to the demands of a new situation. Additionally they made the point that the ability to select, take decisions and make choices is basic to the development of the individual." Parents "were anxious that their children should grow up able to think for themselves, and hence to make decisions. Independence, or autonomy, is what they were aiming at for their children."

Language and communication aims were expressed implicitly by parents who emphasized the importance of social interaction, and by teachers who allotted time specifically for language work.

However, the team found that whereas about a third of their pupils were functioning adequately, the lowest third were able to imitate only single words, or none at all. At 16 years of age one pupil in six had no speech. It should be remembered that the project started in 1973, and most of the older children had spent the larger part of their young lives in training centres under the Ministry of Health, without all the present benefits of education. This is important, for the project team also found that the greatest progress in learning language came between 3 and 6 years, after which development was found to be very slow. Shortly before 16, the age at which many of them left school, there was a language spurt.

SYMBOLIC PLAY AND COMMUNICATION

Direct experience is necessary for the acquisition of action schemata and images which move imperceptibly into symbolic play, and this can never be stressed too much. When young children feed their teddy bears, or pretend that the upturned chair is a car, they are going "beyond the information given" and are entering a world that has no fixed boundaries.[2] In the process they learn that one thing can stand for, or symbolize, another. It is round about this time that most children begin to use speech, aided by gesture, in communicative exchanges. No longer are they confined to well-trodden pathways, but they can venture into unexplored territory which, in turn, can become a starting point for further sallies. They can follow a route that a little girl of my acquaintance used to call a "surprise way" home.

Learning that one thing can stand for another, as in a "Let's Pretend" game, is an important step in developing language. When children use cardboard cartons as tables, beds or pick-up trucks they do so only to meet their present needs, the same carton being used at different times of the day for a variety of purposes. This flexibility reduces the difficulty of letting one thing symbolize another. When learning to talk, or to gesture communicatively, conformity enters. Many gestures are halfway houses, for they indicate their intention. When parents clap their hands and extend their arms they are signalling that they wish the child to come to them. Similarly, toys and pictures bear a resemblance to real things. They are not fully symbolic: a few words too, used only in the early stages of language acquisition, such as "moo-cow" and "baa-lamb" prompt the child to remember which symbol stands for which animal. But why, when "cat" is heard, does the listener know that the animal is being talked about and not the mat it is lying on? It can only be because the convention has been accepted. There is an underlying assumption, which has to be learned, that unlike the pebbles that can be cakes one minute and coins that next we have to agree about the use of words. Children who cause mild affront or amusement by calling every man "Daddy" have still to learn that successful communication imposes constraints. It is interesting that after learning that "Daddy" refers to only one man, their own fathers, children can take a further step and refer to "My Dad", "Your Dad" or Mary's Dad". This shows that they understand that the relationship between themselves and their fathers is equivalent to the relationships of other sons and daughters to other fathers. Children's command of language grows with such successive stages of particularization and generalization alongside the formation and refinement of concepts. This language has to be shared by consenting speakers and listeners. Play allows the child to contrast, at an unconscious level, the idiosyncratic symbolism of pretence and the orthodoxy of language and communication.

Unfortunately, many mentally handicapped children seldom play. Their opportunities for developing symbolization and communication are consequently adversely affected. This is why the value of play cannot be overestimated, and why the importance of teaching children how to play is so frequently stressed. The intervention of adults is paramount in supplying ideas and equipment, and in allowing themselves to be accepting, responsive playmates. It is generally wise to limit the quantity of toys and materials out at once, and to include those that can be used in a variety of ways. This is one reason why building blocks are so popular: they can be banged together, built up and knocked down, or made to represent cars or trains, or whatever the child wants. Children are better able to make decisions, if their choices are restricted, and if, having made their selection, they are helped to explore the consequent possibilities. An essential contribution from the supportive adult is the language which goes with the activity. Another is to introduce the notion of pretence.

In their very useful book, *Teaching the Handicapped Child*, based on the *Parent Involvement Project* at the Hester Adrian Research Centre (HARC), Dorothy Jeffree and Roy McConkey summarize the optimal conditions which characterize the spontaneous play of children as: the presence of tolerant adults; opportunities to imitate adult activities; the right toys at the right time; a few toys at a time; responsive playmates and environments; and four freedoms — from undue stress, to experiment, to make their own rules and from interference.[3]

These add up to opportunities for children to represent to themselves what is, or has been, presented, and to assemble in various and sometimes novel ways their repertoire of skills. Instead of carrying through isolated sequences in the form in which they were learned they can associate previously disparate actions and activities, because they can give meaning to whatever they are doing. They can see more than meets the eye.

When the process of learning is under consideration it is useful to differentiate integration, the behaviour that manifests itself in automatic sequences — what we have called "the well-trodden pathways" — from representation, the level which is concerned with meaning, thought and intention.

NEUROLOGICAL CONSIDERATIONS

Of the thirty-thousand million neurons in the body ten-thousand million are in the brain. The cell bodies of these neurons have many short hair-like fibres projecting from them, called dendrites, and a fibre extending from one side, the axon, which ends in dendrite-like fibres finishing with synaptic knobs. These knobs are separated by only about a millionth of an inch from the dendrites, each forming a synaptic gap. Electrical impulses are transmitted across the gap by chemical (not electrical) activity to the next neuron. The chemical which is released either excites or inhibits the electrical activity in the adjoining dendrites. The synaptic knob and gap are together known as the synapse. By means of this complex process (very much oversimplified in this account) impulses can be switched, co-ordinated and integrated by the way groups of neurons act together. It is thought that as many as a thousand neurons can make synaptic connections with the dendrites of a single cell body.

When the synapse is excited an imperceptible change takes place in the synaptic knob, which is recognized, if excitation is frequent, by a growth in size. This increases the probability of activation, and possibly accounts for the well-trodden pathways. On the other hand the constant interplay of neuronal activity accounts for the permutations that must occur in learning, memory and thought. There are processes in the brain which accompany language and processes that are concomitant with thought, and together these communities of synapses underlie the level of organization which we call representational.[4]

At the representational level the mental activities such as thinking, reasoning, supposing, imagining, applying rules and solving problems are carried out. Because these go beyond the information given — that is, because they are not dependent on whatever is present to be perceived — pondering and reflecting can result from self-arousal. You can close your eyes, dissociating yourself from the most potent sensory input, and plan your weekend, solve the world's problems, or whatever, relying on your ability to call on your own resources. What goes on at the representational level is not necessarily hi-fi: it can be very mundane, but it is your own and can come only from your store of experience.

LEVELS OF ORGANIZATION

In language the two levels of organization can be readily distinguished, for grammar has an automatic-sequential basis, while semantics is concerned with the representation of the content or the message. Both are necessary for communication. It is somewhat like a car journey: a successful one needs an engine and a route which leads to the destination. When children learn to speak they have to acquire the grammar of the language at the same time as they are learning the purposes to which language can be put. Their grammar does not come fully fledged, nor do they have a large repertoire of meanings to express.

Since children's first utterances are single words it is rather odd to discuss them in grammatical terms, for grammar implies sequences of morphemes to form sentences. (Morphemes can be words, or parts of words, which add to meaning such as -s, -ing, -ed, un- or -ly.) Nevertheless, it is sometimes possible to understand the grammatical function of single words, and of the component words of two, three or four word utterances, such as "No supper", "Eat a sandwich" and "Umbrella for the rain" all recorded in one classroom discussion.

Some single word utterances seem to be noun-like, and others verb-like, but then there are words like "there", "more" and "no" which, when spoken in isolation, are difficult to place. However, it is sometimes possible to recognize questioning and commanding, and also that some utterances are stereotypes, such as "bye-bye" or "ta".

Even at this early stage of language acquisition it is useful to record the words the child uses and to classify them, if only tentatively. This sometimes shows up a total or relative lack of verbs in the vocabulary, without which progress to two-word, and even more to three-word, utterances is hindered. The use of verbs indicates an ability to recognize what is happening, a great advance on noticing what is present. This can be seen later on when a child is asked to talk about a picture. The immature response is to name the items, but Donald, a 16-year-old boy with Down's syndrome, when shown a picture of rain coming through the bedroom ceiling, said, "Dad doesn't like the water. Put his head under the clothes so he doesn't see the water. Oh Dad! You've got into a proper mess now."

TESTING LANGUAGE

As a preliminary to treating language delay a number of ways of analysing and diagnosing children's language have been produced, most of them assuming some specialized training and knowledge such as speech therapists and teachers acquire on initial and post-experience courses. These will be reviewed briefly for they have been drawn up as a part of the close study that has been given in recent years to the acquisition of language. When children have difficulty with any or all of the various aspects of communication, knowledge of what to expect is a guide to action. If something is going wrong a test or an analysis may throw light on what is causing the hold-up, and even when the cause cannot be determined there may be a pointer to profitable intervention.

Some English Tests

The Reynell Language Development Scale (RLDS) for assessing very young children listening and speaking has two sections, one to evaluate receptive (listening) and the other expressive (speaking) language. It is especially necessary to explore children's understanding of speech when physical or other disabilities prevent them from uttering, and in other cases to compare listening and speaking skills.[5]

Another instrument has resulted from the work of David Crystal and his colleagues at the University of Reading. This is known as LARSP, Language Assessment, Remediation and Screening Procedure.[6] The emphasis here is on the grammatical rules that govern early utterances. As a companion to this, David Ingram has devised a set of techniques for the collection and analysis of the language of children with disorders of articulation.[7]

Two tests which have been produced at the Hester Adrian Research Centre as a result of several years of working with mentally retarded children are the Language Imiation Test[8] and the Sentence Comprehension Test.[9] The latter, still in experimental form, only requires children to demonstrate their understanding of grammatical differences between sentences, such as singularity and plurality. The former elicits speech. Both these tests help to elucidate the problems of children who experience difficulties in learning language.

An American Instrument

A rather different approach can be seen in the Environmental Language Inventory.[10] In this, James MacDonald and associates at Ohio State University have focused on the context of the utterance, thus emphasizing its meaning and the intention of the speaker. Their semantic-grammatical analysis (as they call a content-form analysis) is particularly interesting when considering the relationship of language to thought. The point at issue is whether thought is possible without language, and in which ways they assist each other. As long ago as 1908 Binet foresaw that the problem of the relationship between semantics and syntax was the key issue in language learning, especially in association with mental or physical handicap. It seems that whereas language is not essential to the development of thought, in Piaget's words, it "contains a wealth of instruments at the service of thought".[11] When you know something you are likely to express that knowledge in words, if you have the words to use. It is sensible to wonder about the conditions under which language assists and shapes thought, and vice-versa, and how this reciprocity is effected.

By implication this consideration has directed the research of the ELI team. Their inventory samples imitation, conversation, and children's language in free play. So that their capabilities can be discovered and their weaknesses diagnosed, every encouragement is given to testers to adapt the content. The guiding principle is that the child's natural meanings should be tapped, and that non-linguistic cues (the objects and actions that the tester uses to elicit responses) should be familiar and appropriate to the subject's age and interests. The child (or adult) is first asked to reply to a question, or to the request, "Tell me . . .". If the response is less than optimal an imitative task is presented and followed by a repetition of the original question or request. (In experimental use the administration is more tightly controlled.) Since 1978 a non-professional instrument has been available — Oliver: Parent Administered Communication Inventory[12] which explains how the stimulus items can be adapted without breaking the three rules: that the substitutions must encourage the same kinds of response as those given in the text; that linguistic and non-linguistic cues are presented simultaneously, and that the child's language is assessed in three modes, imitation, conversation and play.

Children need about fifty single words before being *taught* to combine them. Their earliest spontaneous attempts are usually to put together agent and action, such as "Me push", or action and object, "Push car". These are followed by agent and object, "Me spoon". They have to be analysed in relation to their context: the first two were recorded while the child was pushing a car and the last while eating. Semantic-grammatical forms that follow express location, "Cat chair" or "Go garden"; negation, "Allgone light"; modifiers, "Wet sock", "Daddy car" (possession) or "More milk", and introducer, "This shoe" -- again all needing to be recorded with their contexts.

When the child is able to combine two elements successfully a start is generally made on three word utterances, then on those using four words, and from then gradually (very gradually) to sentences which approximate to adult usage.

From the outset the ELI has been used both for testing and to guide teaching, not only in clinics but also in schools, and in the home where parents join in training language. By 1978 over 130 environmental programmes had been conducted in Ohio, Montreal and Toronto with language-delayed children and adults, the first with six Down's syndrome children. The involvement of parents and teachers who had close contacts with the handicapped was entirely justified. In some cases informal language training became a part of the everyday life of the family, and one mother of a 4-year-old Down's syndrome girl, Barbara, reported that her 8-year-old son told his friend who was playing with Barbara on a swing only to push her if she used at least two words to ask him to! The length of Barbara's utterances improved significantly with these methods.

THE USE OF LANGUAGE

Although this method of analysing a child's developing language is a useful guide to intervention, (as are LARSP and other schedules) one important aspect is not included, for the concentration is still on the forms the child's language takes, and not on the use they are put to. Teachers, who have the opportunity of comparing the behaviour of mentally retarded pupils, know that the most effective communicators do not always show up best on formal analysis. What is it then that they can do?

Communication does not start, or end, with speech, but arises out of the social interactions of family life. Babies and adults convey their pleasure, displeasure, desires and intentions without using words, and by means of these preverbal communications they regulate each other's behaviour. When a mother leans over a cot with outstretched arms and a smile on her face she conveys her intention of lifting her son or daughter and her delight in doing so. The baby reciprocates. One of the saddest aspects of rearing profoundly handicapped children is that these kinds of actions and the pleasure that accompanies them do not bring about the usual baby responses. In the face of apparent rejection it is understandable that the mother gets discouraged. One-sided communication does not flourish without great determination from the able partner. Nevertheless, when non-verbal messages are understood the gap between preverbal and verbal communication can be bridged by adding speech to action. In a similar way the toddler first takes a doll and a sock to mother and tugs at her skirt to get her to put the sock on the doll. If she does so the child's intentional behaviour is confirmed, for mother's behaviour has been correctly regulated. Later on the request may be "sock", "sock on", "put sock on" or "I can't get its sock on" and any of these speech acts may produce the same result.

Besides regulating the behaviour of others children can direct their own behaviour by talking to themselves. In a subtle way this also helps to establish a self-image, for it brings the speaker and listener into alignment. Developing a body-image of the physical entity and the self-image of the psychological entity are both tasks of early childhood, and either may take mentally retarded children a long time.

Taking the listener into account is another skill that has to be learned, for besides directing their own or another's behaviour children need to know how to express their feelings, explain situations, ask for information, promise, persuade, threaten and so on. Just take the single word, "Tomorrow". It can be used to anticipate the following day's excitement, to explain when something will happen, to ask when an event will occur, to promise an ice-cream, persuade the plumber to come or indicate what lies in store unless . . . When mother says, "Is that Daddy's car?" is she asking for information or telling someone to open the garage doors? Some children are better at interpreting and expressing intentions than they are at mastering grammatical structures. Jacky, who seldom produced three-word utterances, had no difficulty at all in organizing the boys on a weekend self-catering holiday. Her social skills and her dogged determination were sufficient. One of her teachers commented, "If anyone can get things going it will be Jacky".

What Jacky was using, informally, was total communication, which can also be introduced formally to children with little or no spoken language. Formal total communication involves presenting manual signs while speaking. Both in the UK and in North America there has been an increase in the use of sign systems in the last few years, or of providing an alternative communicative tool. It has been found to be especially useful when the child is able to join in games of pretence, is physically able to imitate gestures, has some gestures already and lives with a family (or family substitutes) who are prepared to learn the signs too. Experience has shown that reluctant parents become enthusiastic when they find, sometimes for the first time, that they can communicate with their children. The ELI has been adapted for total communication training, and in the UK the Paget-Gorman Sign System[13] and the Makaton Vocabulary[14] (based on the British Sign System) are being used. The Communication Behaviour Rating Schedule[15] gives teachers a straightforward method of identifying how children convey meanings without language, and can be used to guide decisions about which, if any, non-verbal means to use.

A Language Development Chart

There is one schedule that has not been included in this account which has the great virtue that it is written for parents and is couched entirely in non-technical language. This is the language section of the PIP Developmental Charts, and the basis of *Let Me Speak*.[16] Completing the chart, which in itself is a training in how to observe and record, is a preliminary to carrying out simple, practical and relevant learning games to encourage speaking. Many published schemes are unsuitable for children who have, as yet, no speech at all, or only one or two recognizable sounds, but this one starts at the babbling and gesturing stage.[17]

Let Me Speak uses a different approach from either of the two that are most widely advocated. These two, on the one hand, provide a rich verbal environment from which children can pick up the language skills that they need; and on the other hand adopt the principles known as behaviour modification and provide specific programmes for defined tasks, broken down into small steps, each one of which is learned through repetition, with rewards to reinforce the desirable behaviour. The first is only suitable for children who learn easily, though sometimes it seems that teachers have tried to give the richest diet to the children with the poorest appetites. If they could digest so much they could scarcely be called mentally retarded.

There is, therefore, some temptation to choose behaviour modification, but this too has limitations which can be, but are not always, overcome. As we have seen, language and communicative behaviours are essentially general, not specific, though they include specific elements, and it is important that whenever a child is being helped to acquire language it should be in a way that encourages generalization. The games and exercises in *Let Me Speak* are particularly well chosen for they include the fun element of the "enrichment" method and the direction of the structural approach, with suggestions which encourage the use of language, so that both thinking and communicating are related to experience. For example, in the section on prepositions, "Round About", the adult is advised not always to say "In it goes" while playing a game of dropping things in a bucket for "Children often speak more when slightly frustrated". I have experienced this myself. It is sometimes difficult not to let one's mind wander when playing repetitive games, especially with a non-communicating child, and to my extreme surprise on one occasion when I ceased to pay proper attention to a 10-year-old boy he said quite unmistakably, "You're dreaming".

Placing too much emphasis on structure is to plan for the well-trodden pathways, but to forget about the "Surprise ways": in other words, to omit to build in opportunities for applying skills in decision-making or emotion-expressing situations, and therefore not to encourage children in their understanding of the purposes of language and communication.

Nevertheless, a good case can be made out, as Gillian Fenn[18] has done, against verbal enrichment and in favour of planning. She has shown that there is no need for the fun and laughter to go out of learning. Using photographs of the children themselves, their school friends and families is one way of keeping the material interesting and appealing, and of ensuring that the content relates to the child's life. Coloured slides have the advantage of focusing attention, and short sequences on videotape or cine-film have the additional compelling quality of movement. The point is, however, that the structures which have to be learned must not be haphazardly introduced, but need to follow a scheme such as Dr Fenn's own, LARSP, ELI or one on which teaching materials such as *Jim's People* are based.

PROCESSING AT THE REPRESENTATIONAL LEVEL

Processing at the representational level involves first verbally decoding input, that is, recognizing what is seen or seen to be happening, and "telling oneself" what the significance of the material is; second, comparing the experience with what is stored in memory; and third, encoding so that the intention can emerge as output, generally as speech or gesture. Only the final stage is at a conscious level.

In order to differentiate decoding, associating and encoding, Kirk and his colleagues have taken some activities which emphasize each of these processes in isolation from the other two, and organized them as the Illinois Test of Psycholinguistic Abilities (ITPA).[19] For example, if the input is visual and little is needed by way of association or decision-making, decoding ability can be evaluated in the visual reception mode. Such a task would be to look at a picture of a chair and then to find another kind of chair in a picture of a bedroom. Visual association tasks include putting together objects or pictures that are related in some way by responding to the questions (while pointing), "What goes with this?" or "If this goes with this then what goes with this?" Children only need to point to whichever item of an array they choose.

However, if their language skills are very immature they may have difficulty in understanding the question, and their visual receptive skills may need to be explored with the help of gesture or mime. The problem is that when information presented visually cannot readily be decoded, the child may not be able to interpret gestures either. This does not render the attempt useless, but is a warning only to accept at its face value evidence that children have a capability, and to reserve judgement when the evidence is not forthcoming. It is better to say that one has not observed behaviour, than that the child is incapable of it. It is something like drilling for oil: a test which produces some can be accepted with more confidence than one which does not.

There are other forms of input, the main alternative to visual stimulation being auditory, with children listening instead of looking, and responding to the stimulus word directly, or after associating it with their previously acquired knowledge. The complex relationships which we have called integrative and representational are shown in a very simplified form in Figure 6.1. When children can answer questions, ask for what they want, play singing games such as "This is the way we wash our hands" or describe how to make a pot of tea and do so, then they demonstrate their expressive abilities. And they also need a wealth of automatic-sequential skills to support their self-expression.

An Intervention Programme

Jane, an 8-year-old Down's syndrome child, whose language skills and response to a teaching programme have been described by

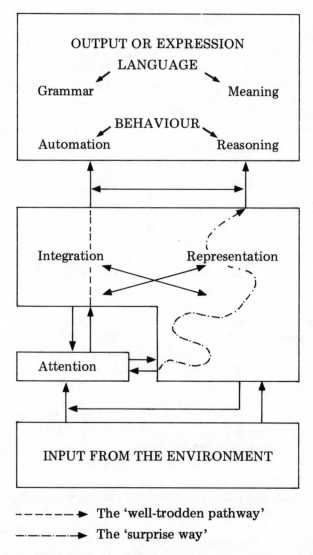

Figure 6.1   A model showing integrational and representational levels of organization

---

Jeffree, had a very interesting profile when examined in these areas.[20] She was better able to take in what she looked at than what she listened to, but was marginally better at recalling what she heard than what she saw. However, the greatest anomaly was in her ability to express herself: using speech she was like a child of 3½ years, but when using gesture she operated like a 7-year-old. Since Jane was able to demonstrate her ability to express herself through gesture, and to imitate, and because she showed an interest in pictures and had the vocabulary of a child of about 4½, she was considered to be ready to improve her immature expressive language. She whispered very short phrases, with fewer verbs than nouns.

Five teaching methods were employed, all using language as an adjunct to a shared activity. The methods were to use pictures of actions rather than of objects, story pictures, moving pictures, drawings by Jane and for her, at her request. Although the language might have seemed incidental to Jane (had she been able to be so explicit), it was by no means accidental; indeed, the objectives were clear and her progress towards them was recorded in detail. The results were very encouraging.

We have to say, however, that the reliable evidence of progress is not necessarily an indication that the methods employed are psychologically sound, nor that the long-term effects of the teaching will justify the effort. In Jane's case it would be safe to expect the gains to be maintained, for the basis of intervention and the methods used were grounded in knowledge and experience. It is so universal a finding that progress is speeded up as a result of intervention, even when the interference is clearly far from satisfactory, that an explanation is called for. The conclusion is that any attention is welcome and affects the outcome, a consequence which is known as the Hawthorne effect (because the phenomenon was investigated at the Hawthorne establishment in the USA).

This effect is both an encouragement to give children extra help, and a reminder to plan the remedial treatment rationally. In Jane's case, and in those reported by Fenn and the ELI team among others, the training followed a careful examination of the children's behaviour in a number of settings, and the programmes which were followed were consistent with what is known about the acquisition of language.

It is easy to get it wrong. A weakness which is seen all too often is to attack the problem face on. Instead of playing or working together and using the opportunities as they arise to introduce the selected language skill in a natural setting, children can be put in front of a doll's house and asked, "What's this?" and "What's this for?" only to get the replies "Bed" or "Sleeping", the single words which the child already has, so does not need to learn. Anxiety drives out reason: over-concern to get the child to use two-word phrases such as "Red car" can lead one to ignore the spontaneous remark "Grandad got car"!

Expressing Relationships

One feature of language which has scarcely been mentioned is the use of prepositions which are important because they show the relationships that exist between objects. Understanding relationships is a key to intelligent behaviour and an indication of cognitive development. Similarly, adverbs and conjunctions present difficulties because, unlike nouns and verbs, they are not "content" words but they have a function in the structure of a sentence. You could miss all the 'ins', 'verys' and 'buts' and still know what was being discussed.

The sensory-motor activities of early childhood prepare the ground, and children extend these experiences by getting into and out of cars, on to or under chairs, and behind or in front of cupboards. Physically carrying out these movements is not absolutely essential to using prepositions but is of great assistance, and if children are non-ambulant they should, if possible, be moved rather than left only to observe movement.

Concurrently children move objects: they use toys which can exemplify spatial relationships, clothes (over your head, round your neck and so on) and cutlery and crockery. Temporal relationships are also demonstrated for the car can go over the bridge *before* it goes round the corner, or the child can watch television *after* tea. Play materials which lend themselves to using function words are of the "world" type, — farms, zoos, and dolls' houses — and Wendy houses and climbing frames. Spatial and temporal relationships are difficult, and the idioms we use such as "*in* time" or "*before* the mast" do not make matters easier.

CONDITIONS WHICH AFFECT LEARNING

Besides knowing something about the nature of language and thought parents and teachers need to know something about the circumstances which specifically interfere with or enhance learning to communicate. These include encouragement to use sound and gesture in social situations.

Round about the time that young children show unmistakeable signs of understanding language (in normal development before their first birthdays) they begin to repeat the sounds they hear, often the last sounds of an utterance. This is so reminiscent of the phenomenon of echo that the practice is known as echolalia. Before this, the babbling sounds they make, which they constantly repeat, include some which are not found in the mother tongue.

When they turn to echolalic utterances these extraneous sounds are gradually dropped, so that only the necessary language sounds remain. These are repeated using the rhythm and intonation of the models that the toddlers hear, the consonants steadily approximating to those of the adults. "Likkle wabbi" ultimately becomes "little rabbit".

Mentally handicapped children's speech development, if they talk at all, follows similar lines at an older age. An interesting analysis of the speech patterns of two Down's syndrome boys can be found in Ingram,[7] which shows in which ways their speech is both conforming and deviant.

When mentally retarded children engage in echolalia it is possible that it receives adverse attention because it is happening at what seems to be an inappropriate age. However, normally developing children actually use far more echolalic utterances at 2½ years than at a year, but this goes unnoticed since there are so many statements and questions as well. Nevertheless, it is unlikely that echolalia would persist for so long unless it served a developmental purpose.[21]

The possibility is that the echolalia of mentally retarded toddlers is not reinforced in the way that "conversation" would be, and that consequently their imitative repetitions are discontinued before their more interesting utterances can get going. We have to ask ourselves if rewarding their babbling and mimicry over a longer period by responding to it would lead them towards more mature speech. The value of imitating the baby's nonsense noises, communicatively, has been demonstrated in practice to encourage language development.

Anatomical studies of the brain are by no means definitive: nevertheless they point to the probability that the complexity of interneuronal connections may be critical. Where there are simpler patterns of dendritic branching than is normal there is probability of mental retardation, and of impaired ability to carry out language functions. However, this research is far from complete, though modern techniques may advance it considerably in the next few years.

Nevertheless, there is long-standing evidence that language function is more strongly based in one cerebral hemisphere (generally the left) than the other, and that injury to the dominant hemisphere has long-term effects on language deficits. The dominance of the left hemisphere in right-handed people suggests a relationship between handedness and language function, but such a connection is certainly a complex one. At present it would be unwise to plan an intervention programme largely on evidence of cerebral dominance, or on what is known about the location of the centres in the brain that are important in language function. However, it is probable that the region where visual, auditory and motor impulses come together and are interchanged is crucial to language learning.

When research into the processes of language in the brain rather than into the structure of the brain is examined, complexity once again predominates. However, it is agreed at present that speech perception is not the same as auditory perception. It is the information-carrying functions of speech that account for the differences. Cora, a Down's syndrome girl, used always to go "Puff-puff" in response to the word "train" and she did so when Jack Train, a radio star, was mentioned. Her auditory perception was reliable, but her speech perception was inadequate. At a more advanced stage children may not recognize sarcasm, or see the point of a joke. If they hear "Peter was knocked over by John" they may not be able to say who did the knocking over, although they would have no difficulty with "Peter was knocked down by a car".

Besides this, auditory perception is not the same as auditory acuity, the latter referring to the child's ability to hear. It is very usual to find that mentally retarded children have poor hearing as well as poor perception. Down's syndrome children, for example, are often deaf or partially hearing in one ear and this adds to the difficulty of the task of understanding what is said. This, when the prevalence of respiratory disorders and catarrhal infections is taken into account, means that teachers and parents should remember to speak clearly. Poor models at best can produce only poor copies, and these may lead to misunderstandings.

Even when teachers speak normally things can go wrong. One mentally retarded boy from a rural area in Northern England was working with his teacher on shapes and was asked to draw a picture of something that was square, which he did. When asked about his picture he said it was a cowfield (an attractive neologism!) with four edges, "But we don't call 'em 'edges; we call 'em walls". It is impossible to imagine what sense he had been able to make of his teacher's explanations of triangles with three edges, and so on.

In general, therapeutic effort may be made more rational by a better understanding of the neurological processes at work in language, though so far most of the alleys that have been explored have turned out to be blind. However, there is some work carried out by Sidman in the 1970s which looks promising.

Sidman found that a severely retarded microcephalic boy

could point to one of eight pictures when it was named, and could name a picture when it was presented singly. He could do neither when the printed word was used. However, he was taught to touch the printed word when he heard it spoken and could then, without further teaching, speak the name when shown the printed word and, touch the correct picture on seeing the word and vice versa. Following up these findings has convinced Sidman that there are stimulus equivalences (that is different stimuli eliciting the same responses) some of which spontaneously cross the sensory modalities (sight to hearing or hearing to sight) and that these stimulus equivalences are basic to language. This is not an entirely new concept, but the experimental backing gives it increased respectability. Rosenberger, who has reported this research, suggests that knowing which equivalences form spontaneously would result in a great saving of teaching time.[22]

ALTERNATIVE SYSTEMS OF COMMUNICATION

In recent years there has been a great increase in the use of sign language with children not thought to be deaf, and schools have been trying out a variety of systems.[23] At the same time the pre-reading schemes known as the *Peabody Rebus Reading Programme* and *Blissymbolics*[24] have been used as alternatives to spelled words. More recently still some teachers have used both gesture and rebuses together, associated with spoken language, some going so far as to produce their own versions of gestures and pictorial symbols. Research findings are hard to come by in such an unsettled area of development, but subjective opinions are favourable.

The signing methods are basically of two kinds; the older ones, reputedly popular with deaf adults, follow their own grammatical rules, while the more recent innovations, the Paget Gorman Signing System in Britain and Signing Exact English in North America, have a structure which matches English grammar. There are similar developments in languages other than English.

Rebus Reading and *Blissymbolics* also exemplify two different approaches to written language. The former, developed initially as an introduction to conventional reading for pre-school children, has been used with mentally retarded pupils as a language development programme. *Blissymbolics*, on the other hand, was invented as an international language based on concepts, and has opened up a number of possibilities for handicapped people.

The interesting thing is that all these methods not only increase communicative skill in the chosen method, but that there is transfer to other modes which could possibly be explained by Sidman's concept of stimulus equivalences. Many parents must have wondered why, when there is so much to do, children should spend time learning to read pictures, or to make gestures that scarcely anyone in the outside world can understand, but evidence of improved communication supports these practices.

It has already been shown that one of the skills that children have to learn is to combine words, but how can they do so if on the one hand they are given single words, or on the other a stream of unbroken sounds which they cannot analyse for themselves. An advantage of *Rebus Reading* seems to be that it simplifies some features of language other than spelling (which is its outstanding contribution). Notably it helps children to separate out individual words. Using the integrative processes of matching and generalizing (every kind of house is ⌂ , just as every kind is spelled h.o.u.s.e and pronounced haus) children learn a rebus vocabulary and combinations of that vocabulary. Teaching methods depend on teachers' experiences and predilections, but one feature is common to all of them: pictures persist; sounds and gestures have no permanence.

It seems possible (but this must be conjectural at present) that the cross-modal integration of visual, auditory and movement inputs, which occurs naturally in most children, needs helping along in some, and that methods which emphasize such a process will prove to be successful where less comprehensive methods have failed.

RESPONSE TO MEANING

Most people agree about the value of speech, or communicative gesture where utterance is impaired, or of using a Blissymbolic communication board in the absence of both speech and gestures. There is less consensus about reading: it used to be thought that the problem lay in helping children to understand what they read. Now we see that the challenge is to find or produce reading materials which match the existing level of understanding, assuming that the mechanics of reading can be mastered. Curricular decisions can best be made by those who know their pupils individually; they are, therefore, out of place here, but principles are in order.

What we are trying to do when giving children tasks at the representational level is to get them to respond to meaning, which is essentially the purpose of learning to read. It is possible (and again one can only speculate) that learning to read, particularly if the material is rebus-like, gives pupils experience in responding to meaning, which, at a below-consciousness level, becomes a "habit of mind". If all the tasks we present to children require no more than an automatic response we can scarcely blame them for "not thinking".

Certainly, in the school with which I have the closest associations I have noticed a difference over the last few years in the pupils, which seems to go hand in hand with the use of Rebus to develop speech and reading. Because the materials lend themselves to individual work in concept development, with a necessity at every turn to make decisions, children have been able to go that much further than matching, ordering and classifying tasks generally take them.[25] For example, they can follow instructions (written in Rebus) to draw circles round all the objects on a page that are not black; or round those that have not got four legs; or round the children who are sitting down. Such an exercise demands a level of processing different from that needed to "colour the triangles red". In the words of Overstreet, "Give a mind something to do and it becomes a different mind".[26]

Another experience of using language which similarly calls on representation is to get children to say in what way two pictures are related. A group of adolescent boys and girls playing this game, and keeping the pair of cards if they succeeded, produced the following "surprises":

Stimulus cards: A tree. A bottle.

Paul:	You can grow a tree in the garden.
Question:	Can you grow a bottle in the garden?
Paul:	No. Both green.

Stimulus cards: A mop. A bar of soap.

Jane:	Soap you wash. Mop all the floor. Wet. With a bucket.
Question:	Why?
Jane:	To make you clean.

Stimulus cards: A candle. A Clock.

Jenny:	No response (Jenny is a very delicate, handicapped girl).
Paul:	If there's a power cut light would go out. Light the candle. Clock would stop.

Stimulus cards: A tap. A seesaw.

Jenny:	In the park.
Question:	Is there a tap in the park?
Jenny:	Get the water.

Stimulus cards: A cup. A saucepan.

Ronald:	Drink.
Question:	What do you mean?
Ronald:	Put milk in. Got handles.

Stimulus cards: A pair of shoes. A letter box.

Donald:	Man wearing shoes. Going out to post a letter.

Stimulus cards: A ladder. A car.

Charles:	Put ladder on car. Climb to a roof. For TV aerial.

These answers may seem immature, but they all show, and the concentration confirmed it, that strenuous efforts were being made to connect two items normally not thought of together. And as E.M. Forster wrote "Only connect"!

The same pupils tried to express their emotions in words, and in response to "What makes you angry?" they answered, "When boys turn their back," and "When Dad gets wild with the dog". In answer to "What do you feel like when you're angry?" Donald said, "Hot".

Their answers to "What makes you happy?" were:

Being in the garden makes me happy.
I took my dog out for a walk. It makes me happy.
Having presents on my birthday makes me happy.
Helping Steve feed the guinea pigs makes me happy.
The sunshine makes me happy.

And in answer to "How does it feel to be happy?" "How does it feel *inside*?" they said:

Being happy makes you feel like driving fast.
Being happy makes you want to run.
It makes you sing.
It makes you dance.
It makes you laugh.
Being happy makes you feel beautiful.

A happy note on which to end.

NOTES AND REFERENCES

1. The Schools Council was founded in 1964 to give a national lead in curriculum development and the public examination system. The first project concerned with handicapped learners was The Curricular Needs of Slow Learning Children (Project Director, W.K. Brennan). The second, which began in 1973, was on the Education of Severely Educationally Subnormal Pupils (Project Director, Prof. Peter Mittler; Deputy director Ken Leeming). The Schools Council Curriculum Bulletin 8, by Ken Leeming, Will Swann, Judith Coupe and Peter Mittler was published in 1979 by Evans Bros. in London under the title Teaching Language and Communication to the Mentally Handicapped and by Methuen: New York as Teaching Language and Communication to the Mentally Retarded. The Cheshire Education Authority, the Hester Adrian Research Centre and the Social Science Research Council Language and Communication Project collaborated with the Schools Council team. The report is the most comprehensive account of language teaching in the UK to mentally handicapped children.

2. *Beyond the Information Given* is the title of a collection of articles by Jerome S. BRUNER 1974, London: George Allen & Unwin. These studies in the psychology of knowing present Bruner's views on cognition, development and education and are of great interest to the serious reader, but are not specifically concerned with mental retardation.

3. The Parental Involvement Project (PIP) was directed by Dorothy JEFFREE and Roy McCONKEY from 1973 to 1977. The *PIP Developmental Charts* are published by Hodder and Stoughton and *Let Me Speak* by Souvenir Press, Human Horizons, Series (1976).

4. For a readable, relevant and more detailed account see *Language, Brain and Interactive Processes* by Roger GURNEY, published by Edward Arnold in 1973.

5. REYNELL, J. (1979) *Reynell Developmental Language Scales* (Revised edition) NFER. A restricted test. N.F.E.R. hire out a film on this test.

6. CRYSTAL, D., FLETCHER, P., and GARMAN, M. (1976) *The Grammatical Analysis of Language Disability*. London: Edward Arnold.

7. INGRAM, D. (1976) *Phonological Disability in Children*, London: Edward Arnold.

8. BERRY, P., and MITTLER, P. (1979) *Language Imitation Test*. N.F.E.R. Some restrictions.

9. WHELDALL, K., HOBSBAUM, A., and MITTLER, P. (1979) *Sentence Comprehension Test*. NFER (revised, experimental edition) Some restrictions.

10. MACDONALD, J.D. (1978) *Environmental Language Inventory*. Columbus, Ohio: Charles Merrill.

11. O'CONNOR, N. (ed.) (1975) *Language, Cognitive Deficits, and Retardation*. London: Butterworths.
    This symposium is the published proceedings of a study group formed under the auspices of The Institute for Research into Mental and Multiple Handicap.

12. MACDONALD, J. (1978) *Oliver, Parent-Administered Communication Inventory*, Columbus, Ohio, Chas. Merrill.

13. CRAIG, E. (1978) "The Paget Gorman Sign System" in T. TEBBS (ed.) *Ways and Means*. Basingstoke, Globe Educational.

14. WALKER, M. (1978) "The Makaton Vocabulary" in T. TEBBS (ed.) *Ways and Means*, Basingstoke, Globe Educational. This is a selected vocabulary from the British Sign System.

15. Appendix E. LEEMING *et al*. See note 1 above.

16. See note 3 above.

17. HORSTMEIER, D.S. (1978) *Environmental Prelanguage Battery*, Columbus, Ohio, Charles Merrill. Also starts at babbling stage.

18. FENN, G. (1976) "Against verbal enrichment" in P. BERRY (ed.) *Language and Communication in the Mentally Handicapped*. London, Edward Arnold.

19. KIRK, S., McCARTHY, J.J. and KIRK, W. (1968) *(Illinois Test of Psycholinguistic Abilities*, NFER. A restricted test. The teaching materials based on this test, GOAL, are not restricted. Distributors: LDA.

20. JEFFREE, D.M. (1971) "A language teaching programme for a mongol child", *Forward Trends* Vol. 15, No. 1.

21. ROSENBERGER, P.B. (1971) "Neurological processes" in R.L. SCHIE-FELBUSCH (ed.) *Bases of Language Intervention*. Baltimore, University Park Press.

22. SIDMAN, M. (1971) "Reading and auditory-visual equivalences", *Journal of Speech and Hearing Research* quoted by P.B. Rosenberger (see 21 above).

23. KIERNAN, C., REID, B.D. and JONES, L.M. (1979) *Survey of the Use of Signing and Symbol Systems*. London, Thomas Coram Research Unit, University of London Institute of Education.

24. HAMMOND, J. and BAILEY, P. (1976) "An experiment in Blissymbolics", *Special Education: Forward Trends*, Vol. 3, No. 3.

25. VAN OOSTEROM, J., and DEVEREUX, K. (1982) "Rebus" in REES THOMAS, *Special Education: Forward Trends*, Vol. 9, No. 1.

26. OVERSTREET, H.A. (1925) *Influencing Human Behaviour*, New York. W.W. Norton.

7

THE SATISFACTION OF LEARNING

"And gladly wolde he lerne"   Geoffrey Chaucer

Sally, who is 15 years old, is trying to build a wall using Cuisenaire rods, (ten coloured sticks graded by length from one to ten centimetres, with a cross-section of one square centimetre). Her task is to find two rods which are equal in length to the brown rod, (8 cm). It is not a task which she finds easy, but she keeps at it because she is continuously encouraged by her teacher. It is doubtful whether she understands what she is trying to do since she chooses rods at random and she registers neither pleasure when the rod fits, nor dismay when it does not. However, half an hour later she is able to recall, without prompting, that she has been building a wall.

Sixteen-year-old Paul, who has come to read to me (not a stranger but, could we say, an "important" visitor in his eyes) tells me before he settles to the task that he has a job to do in his hostel. He interrupts his reading to repeat this, and perhaps applying the principle that "what I say three times is true" he again gives me the same information. Paul reads with understanding like a normal child of about 7½ years.

Hassan, a good-looking, physically fine, active 12-year-old, is not really making progress in school and has been described by the psychiatrist as "inaccessible to education", a description which his teachers agree with, but would like to prove false.

Lucy, another 12-year-old whose progress is disappointing, sits inert, frequently with her thumb in her mouth though she seldom sucks it. She hangs her head and does not appear to take an interest in what is going on. Until six months ago she was a long-stay hospital patient, but is now living with her mother who has recently remarried.

In different ways the behaviour of these four children is connected with the satisfactions that they do or do not derive from learning — that is, with motivation.

MOTIVATION

How can the behaviour of Sally, Paul, Hassan and Lucy be judged? Surely, the only way is by observing their actions: their motives must remain a mystery. Or must they? Is there any way of discovering what prompts their activity or inactivity? Do we know how to encourage them to keep on trying to do what we think is in their interest, or how to change their behaviour when we believe it to be detrimental? The responsibility of parents and teachers to make decisions about what young children and mentally handicapped adolescents need to learn is one we accept.

The simplest way of looking at learning is in terms of the learner wanting something, noticing something, doing something and getting something. However, as we saw in Chapter 2, the phase of signal learning during which reflexes come under control, can scarcely be said to originate in the baby wanting something, except in the most general sense. The human organism, with its very few built-in programmes of action, is not without basic physiological needs of food, oxygen and warmth and the reflexes and the apparently purposeless movements of infancy are appropriate to this fundamental condition. Babies need to kick. It is hard to believe that they want to, until kicking has been experienced and enjoyed.

Nevertheless, it is the experiences of infancy, during which the connection is made between cause and effect, that make it possible for babies to develop expectations that what is to happen is what they wish or otherwise. In previous chapters the words "reinforce" and "reward" have been used because in the early stages of learning it is the consequences of actions that determine their recurrence. But as experience widens anticipation takes over. As we saw in Chapter 4, knowledge brings foresight, which implies not only being able to predict outcome, but to form desires, from which intentions follow. When children want something they will go after it if they know how. This encitement to action is motivation; sometimes it is described as incentive motivation.[1]

What we need to know is how we can encourage children along desirable paths, and discourage unwanted behaviour. If either of these are specific, for example in teaching acceptable toileting, a programme of behaviour modification may be in order, but this is not the topic of this chapter. Indeed, behaviour modification has been given little space in this book for two reasons: to do justice to the research of the past fifteen or so years is a task in itself and, although I acknowledge the contribution that has been made, I find broader motivational studies more fruitful.

MOTIVATION AND EMOTION

When Hassan is said to be a poorly-motivated boy it is not any specific behaviour that is at issue, though doubtless he needs particular help for particular problems, as do we all. It is his overall attitude to social and educative influences that is disturbing. He does not behave as though he were in a classroom, or in the playground or the dining hall. He might be anywhere. He seems to be uninterested in what either children or adults are doing. He might be with anyone. There is little evidence that he notices classroom materials, and he does not join in classroom activities. He has some mannerisms which are slightly reminiscent of autism, but no outstanding problems of that kind and he is toilet trained. He can dress himself, but seldom does so. He understands English, which is spoken at home, but does not speak it. He is far from being inactive, but his activity lacks direction and purpose.

There are at least two ways of looking at his problem. We can examine his upbringing and previous experiences to see what light they throw on his expectations, if any, of success or failure. And we can look again to see whether there are any environmental conditions, such as responding differently to different adults, or to any of his circumstances that might be worth following up.

Hassan appears not to be turned on to notice the features of his surroundings so as to be made curious by them, or to derive pleasure or displeasure from them. He has neither the immediate motivational responses that normally colour integrated behaviours, nor the settled emotional state that is built up by an accumulation of desirable or undesirable experiences. It is as though he lives in a perpetual state of neutrality, indifferent to the consequences of his own or others' behaviour.

Sally, on the other hand, is socially aware. During the wall-building task she frequently turned to look at her teacher. In the ten minutes that I observed her she did not pick up any rod until prompted. However, she read to me with only the usual preliminary encouragement and later recounted to yet another teacher what she had been doing. She made a good job of collecting the coffee cups, and checked to see if I had finished drinking. Her difficulty with the wall-building did not appear to reflect an unsatisfactory emotional attitude to learning, for the general evidence was of a girl willing, though not very able, to learn. In particular she was not excited by the rods. If we examined her previous experiences we should expect to find that she had learned to give and receive affection and approval, a component of the sense of security and well-being that is a basis of a healthy emotional state. Her social worker's report confirms this. I have never tried to but I am sure I could hurt Sally's feelings.

THE PHYSIOLOGY OF MOTIVATION

It is probable that some children are more easily motivated than others, and that some are more emotionally stable than others from birth. We have already seen that impulses are received in the brain by both the network in the brain stem which controls the state of arousal and in the cortex in which responses are initiated. At the same time the activating system in the brain stem involves the hypothalamus in the limbic system, which in turn sets up activity in the pituitary gland and the autonomic nervous system. This leads to the body as a whole responding in an emotional manner. All human behaviour has two qualities: a level of alertness and an emotional tone. It is because of these two states that personality is often described in terms of under or over reaction (see Figure 7.1).

Since any function can be adversely affected it follows that, just as children can be aroused too easily or with too much difficulty, they can also suffer from impaired motivation. Highly complex chemical reactions accompany emotional states; the effect of alcohol or drugs on behaviour indicates how a faulty chemical balance can affect incentive motivation.

Nevertheless, motivation to do this, or avoid doing that, is learned. This is why the study of motivation is central to psychology and education, for we have to learn our motivations, and we learn all the better for being motivated.

LEARNING TO BE MOTIVATED

Sally's dependence on her teacher's praise is an example of a motivational influence which is commonly found in mentally

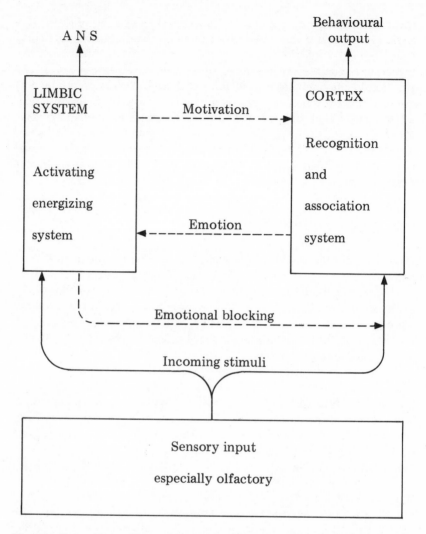

Figure 7.1 The place of the limbic system in learning The energizing activity of the limbic system is not fully understood, but is thought to be related to emotional behaviour and motivation, and also to recent memory

handicapped persons, old or young. They are fortunate indeed if their experiences lead them to trust the adults in their lives, for their intellectual impairments make them vulnerable to inconsistent handling. Incentive motivation is an aspect of the anticipatory behaviour which is the hallmark of successful acquisition of information, for, as we saw in Chapter 4, knowledge brings foresight. It is important that children have opportunities to learn to recognize which events and which of their own actions have predictable consequences, and what those consequences are.

Children often work better for their own teacher than they do for anyone else. It is probable that of all the extrinsic motivators (incentives that are additional to, and not bound up with, the task itself) praise is the most effective. Children come to value the good opinion of their teachers, and mentally handicapped children respond to their approval often into adulthood, when normal students have become relatively autonomous.

However, in addition to praise relating consistently to the children's behaviour, it is necessary for predictive signals to be discriminatory. Unless the signal presages an outcome which can be recognized as either attractive or repellent it has no motivational effect. "Couldn't care less" is no incentive to approach the task, nor to avoid it.

One difficulty lies in knowing what counts as an incentive, apart from the expectation of approval. It is not only a matter of finding out (or guessing) which edible, or piece of music, or hug, or whatever, is the one that incites children's desirable behaviour; it is keeping up with their changing desires, especially when a group of children is concerned. "Let's put everything away so that we can have a story" is fine for the children who want a story at that particular time. Less specific incentives, interspersed with occasional goodies, have a more lasting effect than any system of stars, tokens or similar rewards. This is why I like to see teachers varying their signs of approval, so that their appreciation becomes generalized. Too many ecstatic exclamations must wear thin in time, although in remedial work in the first instance the signal must be quite unmistakeable. Hassan and Lucy, for example, who are as yet indifferent to their teachers' opinions, may need very exaggerated messages of approval, and probably of disapproval as well in Hassan's case, for he does not appear to have realized that there are both desirable and undesirable actions. But as time goes on the changes can be rung, from outright praise to murmurs of appreciation and from hugs and pats on the back to nods and smiles, as the situation warrants.

Being a member of a group can also be an inducement to show what one can do, not always to the good, as the behaviour of crowds sometimes demonstrates. Many teachers dislike competitive activities in school, especially when the class includes children who cannot compete on equal terms, notwithstanding the fact that a competitive atmosphere can be a challenge to try harder. Besides that, ideas foster other ideas, and what children might not think of on their own, they may manage in consort. The "generating ideas" sessions in which the pupils respond to questions like "What makes you tired?" are good examples of how the response of one pupil is an incentive to another.

One school for children with moderate to severe learning difficulties (ESN(M)) had a very attractive incentive. The trunk and branches of a tree were painted on card approximately five feet high and six feet wide, and hundreds of leaves were cut out in sticky paper and distributed throughout the school. Any child who did anything commendable was given a leaf to stick on the tree, and the day often began with a reminder that leaves could be earned. This proved to be an inducement not only to try hard with school work, but to do helpful and kindly acts throughout the day. No leaf was identifiable once it was stuck to the tree, and all the children associated themselves with the tangible evidence of endeavour. There is some evidence to show that if two retarded children are working side by side praising one is an incentive to both of them. This might explain why covering the tree with leaves raised the morale of the school.

Social motivation is only productive when the task can be performed effectively. Thomas, whom I have known since he was a schoolboy, is now in his twenties. He is severely handicapped, being both mentally and physically impaired, and is able, so it seems, to carry out only very simple tasks at an adult training centre. However, Tom can cook. He is a splended pastry maker and very successful with cakes and biscuits. And he knows it. Undoubtedly, the extrinsic incentive of pleasing his family and friends is powerful, but no one would question the satisfaction he derives from the task itself. This intrinsic motivation (or effectiveness motivation or achievement motivation as it is also known) is extremely important, for it adds to the stature of the performer. It is a step towards autonomy, for it is not solely dependent on another's goodwill. The pastry is there to prove to Tom what he can do.

Sally's problem with the wall-building lay in the fact that she could not do it. The task was barely within her zone of potential development, for even with help she was not really coping and as she did not understand what was expected of her she could not anticipate success. Washing up the coffee cups was an entirely different matter. In the early stages of learning a new process children may operate at a chance level, blindly going through incomprehensible activities until the point of the task becomes clear, as we saw in Chapter 3. Bobby has great difficulty in understanding the difference between "How many?" and "How many more?" If he has five bricks and his teacher three and he is asked "How many more have you?" he answers "Five". Until he can recognize this important difference he has to be egged on by his teacher. Soon, it is hoped, achievement will be incentive enough, and he will approach such a task confidently.

Some classroom materials are designed to encourage effectiveness motivation. These are often known as learning-to-learn aids, among which are the well-tried *Flying Start Kit* and *Learning About Number.*[2] The most important feature of these materials is that they give children immediate knowledge of results. This teaches them that decisions have consequences, and is an incentive to look before leaping to a conclusion.

It is sometimes possible to modify teaching materials so that children can monitor their own work. A self-monitored task that is neither so easy that it is no challenge, nor so difficult that it is deflating, is a contribution to learning to be effective. In learning games a chance element as well as the need to make a decision means that the spur of competition can be introduced without always favouring the best players.

Other contingencies can be manipulated. When pupils have to perform two tasks during the course of a session at school, or at home, one of which is preferred over the other, it is better that they start with the one they like less, using the preferred task as an incentive to work on the first one. When this was tried out with severely retarded hospital patients they did fifty per cent better than when the preferred task was given first.[3]

On the whole mentally retarded children are motivated more by extrinsic than by intrinsic incentives, though this may reflect our inability to find enough tasks for them to perform effectively. Paul, for example, presumably anxious about his reading ability, wanted to ensure that I knew about a task he could do, and which carried with it the additional kudos that it had been assigned to him. Anxiety to do well improves performance, unless it reaches such a level that it has a negative effect.

SUCCESS AND FAILURE

As children grow up they become increasingly able to judge their own performance and to be satisfied or dissatisfied by applying their own standards. They become internally controlled. This shows itself in the way they plan their work, and also in the way they are prepared to work for long-term ends. Young children need more immediate gratification. Mentally retarded adolescents tend to remain immature in these respects. Most of them are externally controlled, relying more on the judgement of others than on themselves. Their learning handicaps, which predispose them to experiencing difficulties and expecting failure, give them less reason to trust their own abilities than children who learn easily.

However, if one looks at the research evidence, as compiled by Peter Siegel[4] it is difficult to reach firm conclusions. The general tendency is for mentally retarded persons to be more responsive to reward for success than to absence of reward, or even to loss of reward, for failure. As always "general tendency" is of limited help when you have to decide about pocket money, or tokens, for a particular child.

Children can only be motivated, extrinsically or intrinsically, if the task is within their capabilities and they understand what they have to do. Siegel is critical of much of the experimental work because these precautions have not been reported, and probably not taken. He is also far from convinced that enough care has been taken when deciding on the incentives. However, he quotes one experiment which did set out to discover which of twenty toys would be most suitable to choose as a motivator ranging from a black and white videotape to a free colour catalogue. The subjects were girls and young women living in an institution. The five most popular were a rocking horse, musical box, video-tape from *Sesame Street* (a TV programme for young children) a rocking chair and the coloured catalogues.[5]

These would not necessarily be chosen by other groups, as the experimenters pointed out. The most important finding was that staff who knew the girls well did not agree with each other when guessing what would be chosen, and only the psychologist was able to get anywhere near the actual choices. It seems that intuitive prediction is unreliable. We have to be cautious, therefore, in accepting experimental evidence on the results of rewarding success and punishing failure.

It is safe to say that children can be deceived by praise (we can all fall for flattery) but probably not indefinitely. This suggests that nothing can ultimately replace self-knowledge of achievement, made all the sweeter if others give the credit that is due. Nevertheless, if, as we have some reason to believe, mentally handicapped children are slow to develop awareness of their own achievement, they need us to emphasize their successes and minimize their failures, the reverse of what happens without our intervention. Careful planning of the steps in a learning task becomes paramount, so that our approbation can be justified. If we do not give mentally handicapped children sufficient reason to trust their own abilities we may, in the end, teach them to be ineffective. Opting out is a defensive response, and a protective one. You cannot be made accountable for what you do not do. Success must be a possibility worth considering.

The expression "learned helplessness" was first coined to describe how dogs behave when they cannot escape an electric shock. Since then many experiments have followed to explore the possibility that human beings can also learn helplessness. If there is no way of changing the outcome, motivation is reduced. Looking at Lucy, sitting so inactively if left to herself, one sees her as someone whose self-image does not include effectiveness. The problem is how to make a start on changing her expectations, perhaps even on giving her expectations now that she is living at home again.

It has to be admitted that some of our practices are conducive to teaching helplessness to mentally handicapped children in large institutions, and two American workers have actually devised a scale for measuring it.[6] One of their behavioural tests was to see if the children sharpened their broken pencils or just sat waiting. Similar tests which parents or teachers could easily try for themselves would be to observe what a child does if a spoon is missing, or if there is no chair to sit on, or no towel in the bathroom.

One way of helping children to take responsibility for their own learning is to emphasize the means by which behaviour can be monitored. When children are learning a task they can, as we saw in Chapter 6, direct their behaviour by talking to themselves, and they can check their work in the same way. Teachers can demonstrate this by saying, for example, "Good. That's right because it's red" or "That's better. That fits, doesn't it?" and so on, including. "That can't be right. It isn't red; it's green". This sort of information sometimes gets lost in too much chatter. It is a variety of knowledge of results. Sometimes, as in putting a jigsaw puzzle together, children can "just see" whether the piece is properly placed. At other times, especially in problem-solving tasks at the representational level, it is an advantage to make intentions explicit, so that the children know the goal they are aiming for, and then to confirm, again explicitly, that they have done what was required. Cognitive and motivational factors cannot really be separated, though each can be considered independently, for they interact to influence performance which if it is effective is an incentive to further learning. Learning is cumulative, as we have seen, but we sometimes forget that not-learning is cumulative too.

NOTES AND REFERENCES

1. SIEGEL, P. (1979) "Incentive motivation in the mentally retarded person" in N. ELLIS (ed.) *Handbook of Mental Deficiency*. New York, John Wiley. A summary of research since 1967.

2. These kits of Dr Stott's are distributed by SRA.

3. Quoted by P. SIEGEL (see note 1).

4. See note 1.

5. FAVELL, J.E. and CANNON, P.R. (1976) "Evaluation of entertainment materials for severely retarded persons", *American Journal of Mental Deficiency*, No. 81. Quoted by P. SIEGEL (see note 1).

6. FLOOR, L. and ROSEN, M. (1975) "Investigating the phenomenon of helplessness in mentally retarded adults", *American Journal of Mental Deficiency*, No. 79. Quoted by P. SIEGEL (see note 1).

8

PRACTICE MAKES PERFECT

"Skill is behaviour at its best"   G.P. Meredith

It may seem perverse to suggest that mentally retarded children should strive after perfection which, fortunately, is beyond the reach of everyone. But as we have been reminded by Thomas's pastry-making, even quite severely handicapped children and young people can excel in the performance of certain tasks. Most of us who have known handicapped children over a number of years can cite instances of outstanding attainments. These are often thought of as exceptions to the general rule that retarded children achieve little in whatever they undertake compared with their normal peers.

In Britain one of the first large-scale attempts to dispel the view that next to nothing can be expected of the mentally handicaped was the Slough Project which ran from 1962 to 1969.[1] The application of psychological, sociological and educational principles to the industrial training of mentally retarded school leavers (age range 15 to 24 years; IQs between 15 and 54, with a mean IQ of 36) showed what could be done with comprehensive training. The young people were introduced to workshop practices, including potentially dangerous ones, with clocking-in, fixed breaks, canteen meals and so on in a simulated factory setting. Some of the young people lived in nearby hostels and had additional training in independence.

This attempt, while mentally retarded children of school age were still excluded from the nation's educational services, showed how training could develop latent potentialities in some young trainees. There was little reason to doubt, when the experiment came to an end, that it was possible to teach skills to many young mentally retarded workers. Subsequent experiences in the UK and overseas have confirmed this finding, though we still need to create more and better learning environments for school leavers. The skills that children learn at home and in school should be the precursors of those that will serve them throughout their lives. The rest of this chapter deals chiefly with educating adolescents, bridging the gap between early learning and adulthood, but it must be emphasized that skill learning applies at any age. However, as pupils grow older their need to operate skilfully becomes more pressing.

SKILLS OR SKILL

The word skill and its derivatives are not difficult to use in everyday conversation. Although there might be disagreement over details, expressions such as "a skilled worker", "golfing skills" or "a skilful piece of diplomacy" would not be misunderstood. Each of these implies a task that needs a period of training, or flair, or both. However, psychologists use the word skill more broadly. They are interested in a larger range of activities that a trade unionist, for example, would call skilled or even semi-skilled occupations. Their special concern is to determine the criteria that can be applied to decide whether the operator is skilled and competent or clumsy and ignorant at whatever is undertaken.[2] Because of this it follows that psychologists study the skill that goes into tasks like hammering nails, tying shoelaces, or catching a ball. Such perceptual-motor activities usually receive scant attention from the layman, probably because they are so ubiquitous. Nevertheless, a moment's thought reminds us that the brain has to direct hands skilfully to pick up a pin from the floor, hold a pen or pour from a bottle. Yet the subtle adjustments of fingers and thumbs are taken for granted unless something goes wrong with the performance. What goes right psychologists call skill, and they study to determine what the behaviours that they recognize as skilful have in common.

The Nature of Skill

There are four main features that characterize skill. The first is that behaviour described as skilled is not simple and unitary, which, in any case, is seldom found in human activity. Skill entails the coming together of sub-skills, each in turn supported by others.

This can be envisaged as a pyramid of sub-skills with skilled performance emerging at the peak. More height needs more breadth. Take an activity which obviously requires skill such as dancing, with ballet dancing demanding the greatest virtuosity. This can be broken down into a range of musical and physical skills, and each of these into lower order skills, which would include the abilities of tapping a rhythm and maintaining upright posture, each of which is underpinned by even more basic components. Skill depends on a hierarchy of sub-skills, whether it is relatively rare like ballet dancing or as common as cleaning one's teeth.

The second essential is feedback (discussed briefly in Chapter 4) which enables the performer to adjust his behaviour while behaving. Unfortunately the expression "positive feedback" has crept into the language, when what is meant is a favourable report, or welcome criticism. The concept that is relevant here is that of negative feedback, taken from cybernetics, the study of control systems in living organisms and machines.[3] It is by negative feedback that both over and under-reacting are brought to the desired level of activity by cancelling the excess or wiping out the deficit. A simple example is the way we raise or lower our voices when we see the effect on our listeners. Another is the way we keep ourselves, our bicycles or our cars on course by steering. All skilled behaviour is moderated by feedback of great complexity, and its breakdown has serious consequences. In the muscular system, for example, inadequate or faulty feedback can cause a range of problems from clumsiness to cerebral palsy or other pathological conditions.

It is worth noting that positive feedback in its original cybernetic sense usually leads to breakdown, for a system in which "the more the more or the less the less" operates can be calamitous. It happens when the class is noisy and the teacher shouts, so the class becomes noisier and the teacher shouts louder until . . . Or the child makes few demands, and the adult takes little notice, so the child makes fewer demands and the adult takes less notice until . . .

Feedback can be both internal and external. When it is internal it is an intrinsic, concurrent part of the action, not susceptible to conscious control. External feedback, on the other hand, is an addition to the performance, coming in the form of knowledge-of-results. This may be immediate as it is in a game of darts, or delayed as it is when you taste the Christmas cake you made in October. Results can be self-monitored, or provided by an adjudicator. It has already been noted that teaching materials which incorporate immediate knowledge-of-results are an aid to learning, especially if the child can make his own judgements. Board and card games, frequently, it is true, depending as much on chance as on skill, have this quality. It is unlikely that players would play game after game if they were unable to see how they were progressing. The contrary being the case, they hold the interest of the players for long stretches of time. This is why it is a good idea to add to popular table games an extra feature of something to be learned or practised, such as clock time.[4] As we saw in Chapter 7, feedback plays an important part in motivating learners.

The elaborate tense structure of the English language includes the future perfect, *I shall have written*, *you will have read*, which expresses knowledge-of-expected-results. This is sometimes called "feedforward", for it is essentially anticipatory and predictive, and, one hopes, hopeful, for, like the future perfect tense itself, it represents a time to look forward to, by which a plan or intention will be completed. Feedforward acts at the same level as feedback in operations such as moderating the voice, or preparing to negotiate adverse camber, and has been demonstrated to have a physiological counterpart. At both internal and external levels skilful performers not only modify their behaviour as a consequence of their output, but prepare themselves for the input "To be forewarned", as we say, "is to be forearmed." Feedback, with its corollary feedforward, is the second essential feature of skill. To be ready and set to go is the anticipatory aspect of attention. We encourage it when we show children how to hold their hands ready to catch a ball. Or when we say, "Are you sitting comfortably?" as a signal to be ready for storytime.

The third element has come up many times already: it is automation, the hallmark of integration. Automation suggests automata, robots and the like. However, the automatic components of skilled behaviour are not limited and limiting, quite the reverse. It is the repertoire of sub-skills coming together effortlessly, and often unconsciously, into a complex whole as the result of practice that produces the skilled performance, like a play which is "all right on the night". And like a play, every performance is slightly different.

Habit and Skill

Habit and skill can be confused because they both depend on automation, but habits really are like the actions of automata: they are performed mindlessly. This is not at all the same as the automations which characterize skill. If you answer "fifteen" when asked for three fives "without thinking" this is not because you are mindless, but because at some time in the past you have been mindful, and to good purpose. However, it is possible to produce the answer mindlessly, if the original learning has not incorporated understanding. The difference shows up when the fact has to be applied. Not long ago I met an American Down's syndrome 14-year-old who impressed me as exceptionally well-socialized. He was proud of his ability to count, and volunteered to count to one hundred in fives, which he did. However, he could not tell me that two nickels made a dime, though he recognized them as five and ten cent pieces. This is not to say that he will never be able to use the facts he has learned: it is quoted to illustrate the difference between memorizing something by rote, and committing to memory something which is understood.

In general, habits do not serve as well, because they do not take prevailing conditions into account. Like a clockwork car, they pursue their course irrespective of the table leg in the way. If Wayne had been able to use five, ten, fifteen, twenty instead of being able only to count in fives to a hundred then he would not have come a cropper over an elementary application. (He might not, however, have been as proud of his achievement as he undoubtedly was — and that is not a negligible consideration.) The mind has its part to play in skilled performance however successfully the smooth execution camouflages the effort. Selection of sub-skills and timing are of the essence.

The final characteristic of skill is the consequence of the prvious three: it is productivity. A child who can manage to tie only one pair of shoelaces is not skilful in this respect. It is necessary to demonstrate the ability to tie thick, thin, leather or nylon laces in different pairs of shoes to qualify as a skilled shoelace-tyer. But having acquired the skill there is every reason to suppose that any shoelace-tying tasks would need no further training. The *sine qua non* of skill is that what has been learned in one or more contexts can be transferred to other tasks with little or no further learning.

SKILL AND MENTAL RETARDATION

Because operating skilfully is the culmination of much early learning it is only to be expected that young people whose major disability is a handicap of learning itself will be slow to be skilful. Some may never reach the stage where the sub-skills, the feedback, the automation and the feedforward come together in such a way that skills can be transferred to fresh problems. Inevitably, since learning takes longer for the mentally retarded than for their normal peers, they learn less and some of the methods used in training inculcate habits rather than skills. This is a pity, because there are inherent weaknesses in teaching what Kephart calls "splinter skills".[5] These are performance, tricks almost, which go so far beyond the general level of functioning that they cannot be incorporated into the child's usual range of activities. The aim should be to teach skills so thoroughly that they can be used after an interval without practice (maintained) and applied to a number of different tasks (transferred).

Maintaining and Transferring Skills

For their review, *The Maintenance and Generalisation of Skills and Strategies by the Retarded*, John Borkowski and John Cavanaugh gathered together more than fifty recently published research articles and many other published papers.[6] Their aim was to support and contention that "given optimal training, acquired skills and strategic behaviours of retarded persons are persistent and generalisable", and to present contrary evidence and opinion so as to give a balanced account.

In their careful scrutiny of so much material they looked particularly at the methods used during instruction, both for presenting the problem and obtaining the response; at whether the same methods were appropriately used on similar tasks; and at how suitable these methods were for solving new problems, with or without prompting or additional training. By no means all of the work they reported reached the high standards they required, and Ann Brown (whom they quote) has gone so far as to say, "We know of no studies where, far from attempting to train generalisation, the experimenter has even hinted that this is the name of the game". Understanding the problem of training, maintaining and transferring skills has come a long way since the Slough project, but there is still much to learn about the technology. Currently, work is being carried out at the Hester Adrian Research Centre as well as in many other centres world-wide.[7]

In most of the studies reported by Borkowski and Cavanaugh, children with moderate learning difficulties have been the subjects of experimentation,[8] but one study in which children with severe learning difficulties were the subjects is particularly interesting. In 1977 Vandever and Stubbs reported on two years' work with a group of pupils with average IQs of 46.[9] They were given reading instruction using a whole-word method and during that time there was significant improvement in remembering and recalling words. However, they reported that there was virtually no transfer to an unlearned word list. (If the children had learned to recognize "fight", "sight", "told" and "sold" they could not make up "tight" or "fold".) The authors speculated that a phonics and whole-word combined method might have produced better transfer. At least they demonstrated that their children could maintain their learning.

Unless schools are very favourably placed for experimental work all they can do is get on with their primary task of educating, and they are not, therefore, best placed to quote findings. Nevertheless, the observations and judgements of experienced teachers is valuable, and parents, too, recognize progress when they see it. Doubts about the work of Vandever and Stubbs (only from reading about it, so possibly unjustified) are based on the methods they used to test "strategy transfer". If the pupils had been taught to recognize only whole words they would have needed to work out the phonic principles for themselves. It was not a test of transfer of strategy if no strategy had been taught or learned, but a test of abstraction. We would not expect a teacher who had painstakingly learned the names of all the pupils in the school to guess the name of a new entrant. Unless the child is recognized as another "little Smith", it is impossible.

In schools for mentally handicapped children where a combination of methods is used there is evidence of the ability to tackle unknown words successfully. Donald, for example, seeing for the first time the sentence, "Get ready quickly and you will manage to catch the eight o'clock train" worked out "manage" from first principles.[10] The methods by which he had been taught included word-recognition, but emphasized phonic structure by using *Things Alive* and *Distar Reading*, and emphasized other subskills of reading by using *Rebus*.[11] This suggests that reading skills can be transferred to unknown words so long as the pupils are able to establish and maintain the necessary skill in the first place, and transfer strategies are included in the programme.

Evidence on the effect of feedback on transfer is encouraging. When pupils with MAs of six years were given explicit reasons confirming their successful performance ("Good! You knew that because ... didn't you?") they maintained and generalized their skills.[12] It also helps children to talk themselves through a task they are learning. When the child is being introduced to a new problem, such as "Merry-Go-Rounds" in *Flying Start*, the teacher can emphasize the nature of the task by thinking aloud: "That's a duck's head. I must find its tail. Here's the tail. That's right. That makes a duck, etc." A level of maturity is necessary before pupils use these strategies regularly and consciously, but the foundations of skilled learning can be laid in advance.

Training Transfer of Skills

Borkowski and Cavanaugh reach five conclusions on directly training generalization, based on their reading and their own experimental work. First, they say that behaviour should be trained so that at transfer it is maintained by natural contingencies in the new environment. This might be praise, or wages or other tangible rewards that come automatically as the result of good work. Second, a number of different settings should be used during the learning phase. Children who learned to say "Good morning" to their teacher did not spontaneously greet other adults until they had been taught to greet a second teacher. Third, transfer is most likely if the training situation is similar to the transfer situation. This is worth remembering when setting up simulated work experience. Fourth, pupils need to be told explicitly that transfer of skills is the objective of their training. Fifth, the training conditions, at first free of unnecessary distraction, should gradually be modified by the sorts of distractions that are likely to be present in the real-life situations to which the training is to be transferred. In this respect, putting kitchen equipment cooking facilities into classrooms is a step towards transferring skills from school to home. More able children can bridge the gap between home economics rooms and kitchens at home without difficulty, and can profit from specialist teaching, but handicapped children do not easily make "distant" transfer.

To these can be added a further conclusion based on the work of Alan Clarke, who was intrigued by the evidence that mentally retarded adults acquired new skills more rapidly after they had been engaged in industrial training for a time. This suggested that transfer processes were operating, a possibility that ran counter to the accepted opinions of psychologists in 1966.[13]

In his first series of experiments, with 9-year-old and young adult mentally handicapped hospital patients, he found that there was more evidence of transfer with the 9-year-olds than with the young adults. However, relatively speaking the training tasks for the latter were less demanding than they were for the schoolchildren. He therefore followed up this finding with three more

series of experiments. These were (a) to explore transfer of difficult tasks after six months' delay, (b) to test the effect of making
some tasks for adults more complex, and some for children less so;
and (c) holding age constant (this time 12 years) to test the influence of the complexity of three tasks. He demonstrated that
transfer effects can be found if the first task is more difficult than
the second task. This came out even more strongly with normal
pre-school children.

This seems to be a very important finding indeed, for it is
tempting to give easy problems to solve at the outset, and hope
that somehow the child will take the step to harder examples
without help. Asking children to generalize and elaborate skills
they do not possess is a mistake we all make at times. Grading
potatoes that have been grown on the school plot is an appropriate
sorting task for older children, who have outgrown sorting counters.
They will do this more efficiently if trained to fill sacks with
small, medium or large potatoes and then required to sort them
into sacks of small or large potatoes without further teaching,
than if the two processes are reversed.

This conclusion must not be confused with teaching by
carefully graded steps of increased difficulty, for in this case the
teaching is concurrent. It applies specifically to teaching so that
new problems can be tackled independently.

SKILLS FOR LIVING

Social skills are often stated to be the deciding factor if open
employment is being considered, and they are certainly valued by
parents, whether or no. What is interesting in this context is that
an analysis of social skills shows them to have the same characteristics as perceptual-motor skills.

People who have good social skills have a range of social
behaviours organized in a hierarchical manner, with a substratum
of very elementary everyday awareness of others. Their relationships are moderated by feedback, which comes as actions, reactions
and attitudes of others. Feedforward can be seen in the way they
form expectations of the way their behaviour will be received.
Practice makes them confident and relaxed. These features of
their repertoire of social skills give them the ability to adapt their
behaviour to the occasion. This shows up in their stance, their
speech and in their attitudes to others.

It is not easy to learn whom to trust and whom to distrust,
but the same general principles apply to learning social behaviour

as to any other form of behaviour. However, social learning is particularly difficult because one's social success depends not only on oneself, but on the others who form the social group as well. In adolescence especially peer influence is very strong, but not always desirable. An advantage of having two adults in a classroom is that they can demonstrate good humour, consideration and concern in the way they relate to each other. Parents do the same.

Children can only learn social skills by practising them, and they need a range of settings in which to try them out. These include shops, post offices, bus queues, buses and all places where they come into contact with the public. The give and take of social intercourse helps both the retarded and the normal to understand each other. The great increase in school exchanges is very welcome.

Language and number also share the characteristics of skilled behaviour. They are especially productive, for English words are composed of only forty sounds, and there is no end to the messages that can be generated, while all the arithmetic we do uses ten figures and only a few conventional signs such as pluses and minuses. When children's speech is recorded, transcribed and analysed it is never quite the same twice, notwithstanding the small vocabulary on which the changes are rung. Moreover, as with all skilled behaviour it continues to improve, even after many years, until in old age faculties decline.

Naturally, we make every effort to make our children skilful in at least some aspects of their lives, but it is the investment of the psychology of skill in the behaviour of the educators that pays the greatest dividends. "Disabilities of mind", as they used to be called, may become handicaps because *we* are not sufficiently skilful in our interventions. The laws of learning apply to everyone. The central nervous system does not recognize "us and them". Feedback, with feedforward, is the key: we have to learn to tune ourselves in to the child's learning, and to adapt our methods according to the message we receive: we must learn to anticipate the behaviour that will get us the response we are after. To educate skilfully is a worthy example of behaviour at its best, and like all virtue is its own reward.

NOTES AND REFERENCES

1. BARANYAY, E.P. (1971) *The Mentally Handicapped Adolescent.* London: Pergamon Press. This is a critical account of the project.

2. WELFORD, A.T. (1958) *Ageing and Human Skill*, Oxford University Press.

3. SLUCKIN, W. (1960) *Minds and Machines*, London, Penguin. Negative feedback was first used in radio engineering. It is positive feedback that produces the squeal. In living organisms the term used is homeostasis which expresses the tendency to equilibrium.

4. Among the published games for teaching telling the time are those in *Maths Activity Kit Three*. These inventions of DR D. STOTT incorporate immediate knowledge-of-results. Distributed by SRA.

5. KEPHART, N.C. (1960) *The Slow Learner in the Classroom*, Columbus, Ohio, Charles Merrill.

6. BORKOWSKI, J. and CAVANAUGH, J. (1979) "The maintenance and generalisation of skills and strategies by the retarded" in N. ELLIS (ed.) *Handbook of Mental Deficiency*. New York, John Wiley.

7. Edward Whelan has been directing a project at HARC for the past four years (1977–81) on a total curriculum for adult training centres. This should be published shortly. In the USA Oliver Kolstoe, Professor of Special Education at the University of Northern Colarado, is working on behalf of the handicapped on the National Advisory Council for Vocational Education. There are also research programmes at the University of Washington, and in Canada, at Calgary, among many others of which I do not have first-hand knowledge.

8. These are called Educable Mentally Retarded (EMR) and are comparable to our ESN(M) (Moderately Educationally Sub-Normal). The equivalent of ESN(S) (severely ESN) is Trainable Mentally Retarded (TMR).

9. VANDEVER, T.R. and STUBBS, J.C. (1977) "Reading retention and transfer in TMR students", *American Journal of Mental Deficiency*, No. 82, quoted in BORKOWSKI and CAVANAUGH (see note 6).

10. This is a sentence from the *Salford Sentence Reading Test* by G.E. BOOKBINDER, published by Hodder and Stoughton Educational (1976).

11. *Things Alive* and *Distar Reading* are published by SRA. *Rebus* is published by Educational Evaluation Enterprises.

12. FIELD, D. (1974) "Long-term effects of conservation training with educationally subnormal children", *Journal of Special Education*, Vol. 8, quoted by BORKOWSKI and CAVANAUGH (see note 6).

13. CLARKE, A.M. and CLARKE, A.D.B. (1974) "Experimental studies: an overview", in A.M. CLARKE and A.D.B. CLARKE (eds.) *Mental Deficiency: The Changing Outlook*, (3rd edition), London, Methuen.

9

THE MANAGEMENT OF LEARNING

"Saying again,
Unless you teach me I shall not learn"   Samuel Beckett

In previous chapters aspects of the learning process have been discussed largely in isolation from each other. The process is, however indivisible while functioning. Comprehending the totality demands understanding over and above knowing about the components.

From experience I know that a visual model informs some people, but confuses others. For this reason I suggest that if you are one of the latter you ignore the model in Figure 9.1 and go straight on to "Using the model". In any case a model which is designed to simplify a complex situation can only be a simplification. The details which are really the most exciting and illuminating have been filtered out.

The one given in Figure 9.1 is derived from many sources, starting from those given by Kirk as a rationale for IPTA.[1] An elaboration of this can be found in Myers and Hammill[2] but as it stands this model has been put together over a number of years with modifications to express developing insights.

A MODEL OF THE LEARNING PROCESS

The first thing to observe is that no outside energy (such as light or sound waves) enters the central nervous system. Receptors (eyes, ears, finger tips and so on) accept input and transmit it to the brain where the central processes take place which issue in the actions we call responses or output or, in general terms, behaviour.

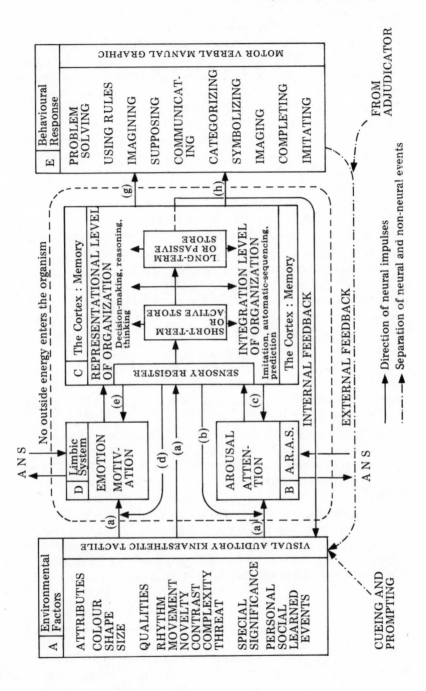

Figure 9.1   A learning model

The second is the number of feedback circuits within the brain, also the external feedback loop, which represents knowledge of results. This has been shown (-.-.-) to be self-monitored and also adjudicated by an outsider, who could be a parent or a teacher. It is not necessarily given and received immediately. The third is that environment includes the automatic nervous system, which serves the organs of the body and the endocrine glands.

Now for the learning process: factors in the environment (A) alert the organism, but it is the organism itself which selects from the possible input (a).

Attention is maintained through the arousal system in the Ascending Reticular Arousal System (B). The feedback loops between this and the cortex (C) are shown as (b) and (c). Loop (b) inhibits alertness while (c) brings about increased arousal.

Integrative processes are shown in the lower half of C. These are imitation, automatic-sequencing and prediction.

Decision-making processes are shown in the upper half of C. There is no anatomical justification for separating them, but there are sound psychological reasons for differentiating those actions which we do "without thinking" and those which require us to reflect.

The limbic system is shown at D. This is a driving force, closely involved in motivation and memory and with the autonomic nervous system. Feedback loops between the limbic system and the cortex are shown at (d) and (e).

The memory bank is shown as a consequence of processes in the cortex. It is useful to distinguish between transient and permanent memories, so the sensory register and the short-term or active store and the long-term or passive store are both shown. The many interconnections in the cortex are represented by arrows.

The assumption that central processes occur which determine behavioural output is based on the experience that when strategies are affected by intervention behaviour is predictably altered. Behavioural output can be at the simple level of imitating or at the higher levels up to using rules and solving problems. This is shown at E.

Behaviour can have both an integrative and a representational aspect. Language, for example, has automatic-sequencing in phonology (the way sounds follow each other,) and in syntax (the way words follow each other). Meaning, intention and thought are representational. Cooking, too: chopping, beating, stirring are perceptual-motor skills but to prepare a dinner decisions have to be made, including how finely to chop and so on. The arrows (g) and (h) indicate the two levels of processing that enter into behaviour.

The input (A) shows that there are a number of sensory modalities, namely visual, auditory, kinaesthetic, tactile, olfactory and gustatory. The output (E) shows that behaviour is essentially motor, for verbal, manual, and graphic behaviour are varieties of movement.

Finally, it must be reiterated, even at the risk of irritating, that the model is a very simple description indeed of an exceedingly complex organization.

Using the Model

Models of the curriculum generally show aims and objectives; learning experiences leading to their fulfilment; methods, organization, materials; and evaluation leading if necessary to a revision of any or all of them. The learning model fits into such a curriculum model (see Figure 9.2) and demonstrates the central role of the psychology of learning and of child development too.

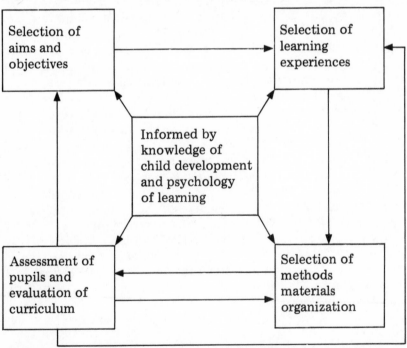

Figure 9.2   The central position of the psychology of learning in a curriculum model

It was suggested in Chapter 7 that the simplest description of the learning process was of wanting, noticing, doing and getting. This is, however, not a useful way of thinking about the teaching—learning relationship for it is much too general to be applied to particular occasions. To some extent this must be true of all such descriptions. However, in practice, the learning model has been a guide to action, both in planning learning experiences and in evaluating learning materials. In the first place is attention to the factors in the environment, both to alert the learner and to keep up the necessary level of arousal. We know from the work of Zeaman and House (see Chapter 3) that breakdown in acquisition may be in the attentional phase, unless sufficient time is given for the learning phase to be reached. This indicates a need to organize the children's task in such a way that their attention is attracted and held, and that the cues, prompts and encouragement the teachers give them are continued until the children realize what is relevant.

The model also shows that the limbic system provides the energy or motivation, without which behaviour cannot be sustained. It also shows that motivation is not just a transient thing, but that, by interacting with the cortex, motivational patterns are formed which influence later learning. The emotions and attitudes which are learned and stored can be the sources of endeavour and enterprise, or , if adverse, barriers to further learning. Incentive or effectiveness motivation, learned and stored in the memory, is so important that whenever children are being introduced to a new learning task the pleasurable aspects of if must never be omitted.

The third step is to ensure that the necessary integrated skills are established before expecting the higher order of cognitive skills, thinking, reasoning and so on, to be available. In the *Rebus* programme as published, matching, sequencing, closure, generalizing and figure-ground problems are included, — all forms of integrated behaviour, and these have been tackled successfully by mentally handicapped pupils. With these skills they are able to compose captions to pictures and to write original sentences which convey a message. The link between integration and representation is prediction, for it is the ability to foresee consequences that lifts behaviour onto the higher plane. This is why it is important to include closure tasks in teaching. A closure task is one in which gaps are filled, such as $2 + — = 5$ or "Betty went to the —— to see the monkeys".

The model also indicates that integration and representation work in harmony and that meaning and intention must never be overlooked. The ability to perform some act perfectly, but without knowing when it is needed, is a relatively useless acquisition. This can be seen when teachers help children to "do the work" without helping them to learn, for learning at its best includes understanding what is to be done, not following instructions blindly.

There is also the question of memory. As we saw in Chapter 5, mentally handicapped young people do not spontaneously use the strategies that most 9-year-olds easily take on board. However, the painstaking work of Herriot and his colleagues has demonstrated that mnemonic strategies are available to the mentally retarded, but that they cease to use them when the instructions to do so are withdrawn. What we do not know is whether the mentally retarded would profit from a much longer span of being instructed to rehearse, organize or elaborate. We know that they needed many trials before they realised what they were expected to do in the experiments of Zeaman and House. Certainly no harm can be done by including in the teaching programme opportunities as they arise to remind pupils to use mnemonic strategies. Of these, probably the most important is realizing that remembering is part of the task. Intending to remember is crucial.

The last component is the behavioural response, and since this can be observed it does not raise the theoretical problems associated with the assumptions that have to be made about attention, motivation, memory, integration and representation. It is important to ensure that different modes of response are included. It is also important to ring changes within the selected mode. For example, in a task in which numbers of objects have to be matched to numerals it is important also that children should match numerals to the number of objects. It is especially important to include the concept of negation or non-existence. Children who are asked to colour the squares yellow can also be asked to colour the shapes which are not squares, or to colour all the shapes except the circles. Understanding is developed when the range of content is relatively narrow, but the variations within it are fully exploited.

When children can see for themselves that what they have done is right, or when the information is given immediately, they generally are happy to stick at the task. Uncertainty may produce anxiety, dislike of the task or one of the various forms of avoidance. This includes uncertainty about the reactions of parents and teachers. The external feedback loop, therefore, represents an essential element of the learning process. In choosing classroom equipment, games and tasks that can be checked by the children themselves should be chosen whenever possible but adults also need to show their interest in the children's activities. The last guide to action that the model suggests is negative: because of the link between the central nervous system and the autonomic nervous system (ANS) it is sometimes possible to observe by a child's appearance — changing colour for example — that a situation is distressing. When this is so, the obvious thing to do is to change or modify the learning task, and when re-presenting it to ensure that success is within reach, by breaking down the steps. Tasks must challenge the pupils, for no learning can take place unless they do; but the pleasure of learning cannot be experienced from a task at which a child can only fail. After the episode in which Sally had difficulty with Cuisenaire rods it was decided, for example, to go back to a matching task of much less complexity before introducing the equivalence task again.

GOALS AND TASKS

When a parent or teacher knows what a child can do it is possible to set realistic goals. Then the specific tasks have to be chosen, and presented in such a way that none of the foregoing elements of the learning process are omitted. The things which the educator can directly manipulate are external, and these should be selected carefully, so that interest never flags for long.

There are, however, many things to manage, especially in a classroom where the needs of the children are sure to be multifarious. This means that foresight, and careful preparation are necessary, and also that the ability to think on one's feet is essential. The classroom should be organized so that the most able, if not all, of the pupils can get what they need, and put it away when they are finished. This reduces the load on the teacher and teaches the children self-reliance, so both profit. A well-planned classroom helps children to classify the equipment and to remember where to put it.

An essential element, which receives more attention today than it did some years ago, is record keeping, so that the child's progress can be regularly monitored. Some schools have a scheme which forces them to review the progress of every child at regular intervals. In some cases the report is followed by specified teaching commitments. The child's progress in these tasks has to be discussed at the following case conference. When parents are informed and involved they can play their part. The objectives, for example, might include some aspect of undressing and dressing for PE, and in this the co-operation of parents is obviously valuable. In more strictly academic tasks it is equally important that parents should know what the teachers intend, and teachers need the information that only parents can give them.

Tasks can be performed at different levels of mastery, and it is important to realize this and to decide on the appropriate level. For some children learning that bus tickets must be paid for is enough; for others the amount the regular journeys cost will be possible; for others the notion, and perhaps the amount, of change can be tackled. Time between steps for assimilation, consolidation and generalization must be given.

WORK AND PLAY

It is a cliché to say that play is children's work, but a true one, nevertheless. If one examines a game such as Lotto (Bingo), one can see that the aspects of learning which have been selected as especially important are all exemplified. Attention can be caught by the appearance of the Lotto card; it can be held by keeping fairly short the intervals at which each child is involved; the chance element is motivating; the number of repetitions reinforce the original learning; the input can be visual or verbal and the output matching. Knowledge-of-results is immediate. When choosing playthings parents can ask themselves whether they will provide opportunities for repeated manipulation; if they can be used imaginatively; if they will encourage language, and so on.

So far the notion of overlearning has not been mentioned, but this is a very important matter, especially for children who find learning difficult and whose achievement may slip away unless precautions are taken. Overlearning is the term given by psychologists to what a learner is doing when practising beyond the point of "just learning". It can readily be seen that games are excellent for overlearning. Dominoes, for example, can be a vehicle for practising colour concepts, number, time, categories (dogs, furniture etc.) at various levels of difficulty over and over again. It is impossible to think of any game that does not enforce repetition, and so give opportunities for overlearning. We sometimes forget that children who are ready for schooling at 5 years of age bring with them a wealth of overlearned skills and knowledge. We cannot make good the retardation of our children whose handicap is a handicap of learning by giving them just enough practice to reach the standard we desire. We, and they, have to stick at the task much longer than that.

CONCLUSION

What may not have come through forcibly enough is that learning should at least be enjoyable and at best be fun. Since the aim of this book has not been to discuss what should be learned many of the interesting things that children do at home and in school have not been mentioned.[3] Instead my concern has been to illuminate how to learn, keeping the examples as relevant and uncontroversial as possible. I am convinced that although no cures for mental retardation are in sight we are justified in believing that with more skill on our part mentally handicapped persons could live fuller and more rewarding lives. Without opportunities to participate in the everyday life of the home, to engage in worthwhile activities and to enjoy art, music or movement however simply presented[4] our mentally handicapped friends and relations miss more than some of them need to do. Even though little of what I have written will be helpful to parents and teachers of the most profoundly handicapped I am cautiously optimistic that more understanding of what happens when a person learns will help us to teach many of the children in our schools to better purpose.

The more complex a task is, the greater the range of ability to perform that task. Bringing up children and educating them are among the most complex tasks one can envisage. It is not surprising therefore that occasionally a genius of a teacher turns up, like Helen Keller's, or that sometimes we meet with disaster. Most of us however, parents or teachers, are more or less all right, and better in some ways than in others. In her introduction to *Teaching Language and Communication to the Mentally Handicapped* Mary Warnock wrote, "To educate a child is to help him in progress; but there can be no progress without clear direction". The same goes for teachers and parents. All of us, given clear direction, can make progress towards being better than we are.

In the past twenty or so years, since, shall we say, the first edition of Clarke and Clarke's *Mental Deficiency: A Changing Outlook* was published in 1958, there has been an immense amount of research, many conferences, courses, articles and books. So much output is impossible to summarize but some clear directions have emerged. With these it should be possible to understand more and to teach better. After all, we expect handicapped children to make an effort. That is the least they can expect of us.

NOTES AND REFERENCES

1. KIRK, S.A. McCARTHY, J.J. and KIRK, W.D. (1968) *Illinois Test of Psycholinguistic Abilities* Urbana, University of Illinois Press.
2. MYERS, P.I. and HAMMILL, D.D. (1969) *Methods of Learning Disorders*, New York, John Wiley and Sons Inc.
3. *In Search of a Curriculum*, by the Staff of Rectory Paddock School published by Robin Wren Publications, 2 Merrilees Road, Sidcup, Kent (1981), deals very thoroughly with the curriculum of an ESN (Severe) school.
4. For books dealing with the teaching of art, music, movement and drama see the list of books for further reading.

FURTHER READING

ATTACK, S. (1980) *Art Activities for the Handicapped*, London, Souvenir Press.

BROOKS, B. (1978) *Teaching Mentally Handicapped Children*, London, Ward Lock.

BRUNER, J., JOLLY, A. and SYLVA, K. (1976) *Play — Its Role in Development & Evolution*, London, Penguin Books.

COOPER, J., MOODLEY, M. and REYNELL, J. (1978) *Helping Language Development*, London, Edward Arnold.

CRYSTAL, D. (1979) *Working with LARSP*, London, Edward Arnold.

CUNNINGHAM, C., and SOPER, P. (1978) *Helping your Handicapped Baby*, London, Human Horizons, Souvenir Press.

GAGNÉ, R.M. (1970) *The Conditions of Learning*, London, Holt, Rinehart & Winston.

GURNEY, R. (1973) *Language, Brain and Interactive Processes*, London, Edward Arnold.

HANSON, M. (1977) *Teaching Your Down's Syndrome Infant*, Baltimore, University Park Press.

HILL, W.F. (1963) *Learning: A Survey of Psychological Interpretations*, London, Methuen.

HOGG, J.H. and MITTLER, P. (eds.) (1980) *Advances in Mentally Handicap Research*, London, Wiley.

JEFFREE, D.M. and McCONKEY, R. (1976) *Let Me Speak*, London, Souvenir Press.

JEFFREE, D.M., McCONKEY, R. and HEWSON, S. (1977) *Let Me Play*, London, Souvenir Press.

JEFFREE, D.M., McCONKEY, R. and HEWSON, S. (1977) *Teaching the Handicapped Child*, London, Souvenir Press.

KIERNAN, C., JORDAN, R. and SAUNDERS, C. (1978) *Starting Off*, London, Souvenir Press.

LEEMING, K., SWANN, W., COUPE, J. and MITTLER, P. (1979) *Teaching Language and Communication to the Mentally Handicapped*, Schools Council Curriculum Bulletin, London, Evans/Methuen Educational.

McCONKEY, R. and JEFFREE, D.M. (1981) *Let's Make Toys*, London, Souvenir Press.

O'CONNOR, K. (1968) *Learning: An Introduction for Students of Education*, London, MacMillan.

SHERIDAN, M. (1977) *Spontaneous Play in Early Childhood*, London, NFER.

TILLEY, P. (1975) *Art in the Education of Subnormal Children*, London, Pitman.

TURNER, J. (1975) *Cognitive Development*, London, Methuen.

UPTON, G. (ed.) (1979) *Physical and Creative Activities for the Mentally Handicapped*, Cambridge, CUP.

WARD, D. (1976) *Hearts and Hands and Voices*, Oxford, OUP.

WARD, D. (1979) *Sing a Rainbow*, Oxford, OUP.

WEDELL, K. (1973) *Learning and Perception — Motor Disabilities in Children*, London, Wiley.

WHELAN, E. and SPEAKE, B. (1979) *Learning to Cope*, London, Souvenir Press.

INDEX